DaVinci Resolve 18

DAVINCI
RESOLVE
EDITING
STEP-BY-STEP
INSTRUCTIONS

Timothy Sharkey, MFA

Deus Ex Machina
CHICAGO
2024

PRINTED IN THE UNITED STATES OF AMERICA

9 8 7 6 5 4 3 2 1

CONTENTS

———

PREFACE...1

INTRODUCTION 2

USER INTERFACE 3

VIEW 6

    CLIP INFORMATION (METADATA)...6
    SHOW / HIDE PANELS 6
    ACTIVATE / DEACTIVATE PARAMETERS...7
    MAXIMIZE SCREEN REAL ESTATE 7
    RED FOCUS LINE 7
    FULL SCREEN VIEW 7
    BYPASS EFFECTS 8
    BEFORE / AFTER VIEWS..8
    BROADCAST SAFE AREAS...8
    DUAL MONITORS 9

NAVIGATE 10

    WORKSPACES...10
    WORKSPACE NAVIGATION TOOLBAR 10
    WORKSPACE NAVIGATION TEXT LABELS 10
    RIGHT–CLICKING 11
    KEYBOARD SHORTCUTS 11
    HISTORY WINDOW 11

MEDIA POOL 12

    SHOW / HIDE MEDIA POOL 12
    VIEW OPTIONS..12
    DISPLAY MEDIA ASSETS IN ORDER..12
    EDIT INDEX 13
    IMPORT MEDIA..13
    BINS...14
    3 KINDS OF BINS 14

Contents

ADD A BIN 14

RENAME A BIN 14

CHANGE A BIN'S COLOR 14

SEPARATE BIN WINDOW 14

POWER BINS...14

SOURCE VIEWER..16

PREVIEW A VIDEO CLIP...16

OPEN A VIDEO CLIP 16

PLAY / PAUSE A VIDEO CLIP 17

SHOW A VIDEO CLIP FROM A TIMELINE 17

SINGLE VIEWER MODE 17

IN / OUT POINTS...17

TIMELINE 19

MULTIPLE TIMELINES 19

CREATE A TIMELINE...19

DUPLICATE A TIMELINE 20

ZOOM 20

ZOOM TO FIT...21

FULL-WIDTH TIMELINE 21

BIG TIMECODE WINDOW 21

PLAYBACK POST ROLL...21

SCROLL...22

MOVE PLAYHEAD TO START OF VIDEO CLIP 22

MOVE PLAYHEAD TO END OF VIDEO CLIP................22

SELECT ALL VIDEO CLIPS AFTER PLAYHEAD 22

SELECT ALL VIDEO CLIPS BEFORE PLAYHEAD 23

NUDGE PLAYHEAD 23

NUDGE A VIDEO CLIP 23

PLAY AROUND A SELECTION 23

UNDO / REDO 23

DISPLAY OPTIONS (FOR VIDEO CLIPS)....................24

CHANGE A VIDEO CLIP'S COLOR 24

LOCATE A VIDEO CLIP FROM TIMELINE................24

SHOW USED VIDEO CLIPS..25

MARKER 25

FLAG 25

DEACTIVATE A VIDEO CLIP 26

DELETE A VIDEO CLIP 26

CREATE A GAP 26

FOCUS SELECT A VIDEO CLIP...................................27

FADE IN / OUT 27

DISPLAY OPTIONS (FOR TRACKS) 27

TRACK HEIGHT 27

INCREASE AUDIO TRACKS AREA 28

CHANGE A TRACK'S COLOR 28

ADD A NEW TRACK...28

DELETE A TRACK 28

RENAME A TRACK 28

MOVE A TRACK UP / DOWN 28

LOCK A TRACK 28

Contents

EDITING BASICS 29

    ROUGH CUT...29
    FINAL CUT 29
    3 STEPS IN VIDEO EDITING 29
    ADD VIDEO CLIPS TO A TIMELINE............................29
    DESTINATION TRACK...32
    MOVE VIDEOS IN A TIMELINE 33
    SNAPPING 33
    SLIP EDIT 34
    SLIDE EDIT 34
    COPY A VIDEO CLIP 34
    DELETE A VIDEO CLIP..34
    MOVE A VIDEO CLIP TO A DIFFERENT TRACK...........34
    ADD A GAP 35
    3 RESIZING TOOLS 35
    RESIZE VIDEO CLIPS 35
    ROLL EDIT 36
    RIPPLE EDIT 37
    NUDGE EDIT POINT (2-UP DISPLAY) 37
    TOP / TAIL EDITS 38
    JKL EDITING...38
    SPLIT A VIDEO CLIP 38
    COMPOUND CLIP 39
    PLAY AROUND AN EDIT POINT 39

EDITING CONCEPTS..40

    CONTINUITY EDITING 40
    PARALLEL EDITING 40
    JUMP CUT 41
    MONTAGE 41
    KULESHOV EFFECT 41
    MISE EN SCENE 42

EDITING TECHNIQUES..43

    CUT ON A BLINK 43
    ENTRANCES AND EXITS 43
    PUNCH-IN...43
    B-ROLL 44
    RADIO SCRIPT 44
    SPLIT EDITS 44

CAMERA SHOTS EDITORS NEED.......................................46

    MASTER SCENE TECHNIQUE 46
    COVERAGE 46
    REACTION SHOT 47
    REVERSE ANGLE SHOT..47
    SCREEN DIRECTION...47
    SEGWAY / BRIDGE SHOT 47
    NATURAL WIPE..47
    180 DEGREE RULE..48
    THE FIVE C'S OF CINEMATOGRAPHY 48

Contents

TRANSITIONS..49
    PREVIEW A TRANSITION 49
    ADD A TRANSITION..49
    DEFAULT TRANSITION 50
    CHANGE DEFAULT TRANSITION.........................50
    CORRECT A BROKEN TRANSITION 50
    CORRECT A ONE-SIDED TRANSITION 51
    COPY A TRANSITION..51
    FAVORITE A TRANSITION 51
    CUSTOMIZE A TRANSITION.................................52

TITLES...53
    PREVIEW A TITLE...53
    ADD A TITLE..53
    ADD AN EFFECT TO A TITLE................................54
    TEXT MASK SIMULATION 55
    FADE A TITLE IN / OUT 55
    CUSTOMIZE A TITLE...56
    TRANSPARENT BACKGROUND 56

VIDEO TRANSFORMATIONS...................................58
    AUTO COLOR...58
    SHARPEN 59
    STABILIZE..60
    WIDESCREEN 61
    TRANSFORM CONTROLS.......................................61
    DYNAMIC ZOOM 62
    BLEND MODES 63
    CHANGE A VIDEO CLIP'S SPEED........................64
    CHANGE A VIDEO CLIP'S SPEED (INSPECTOR) 65
    FREEZE FRAME...65
    REVERSE A VIDEO CLIP 65
    RETIME A VIDEO CLIP 66
    RETIME PROCESSING (RENDERING)....................66
    SPEED RAMP 67
    SPEED RAMP CURVES 68

EFFECTS 70
    SEARCH AN EFFECT 70
    PREVIEW AN EFFECT...70
    ADD AN EFFECT 71
    REMOVE AN EFFECT..71
    ON SCREEN CONTROLS...71
    EFFECT PARAMETERS..72
    TOGGLE AN EFFECT ON / OFF..............................72
    REORDER EFFECTS 72
    FAVORITE AN EFFECT...72
    CUSTOMIZE AN EFFECT 72
    RENDER AN EFFECT...73
    EFFECT ON AN ADJUSTMENT CLIP 73
    EFFECT ON A TITLE..74
    KEYFRAME AN EFFECT 74

Contents

SHOW VIDEO CLIPS WITH EFFECTS 76
PASTE ATTRIBUTES 76
REMOVE ATTRIBUTES..76
THIRD PARTY EFFECTS...76
GREEN SCREEN 76
DIGITAL GLITCH 77
FAUX LENS FLARE 78
MIRRORS 78
KALEIDOSCOPE 79
INVERT COLOR 79
GAUSSIAN BLUR...79
VIGNETTE..80
DOUBLE EXPOSURE 81
ALPHA CHANNELS..81

KEYFRAMES..82
KEYFRAME A VIDEO CLIP...82
NAVIGATE KEYFRAMES 83
REMOVE A KEYFRAME..83
DELETE ALL KEYFRAMES 84
KEYFRAME INTERPOLATIONS 84
KEYFRAME EDITOR..84
KEYFRAME EDITOR'S FUNCTIONS..85
CURVE EDITOR 86
CURVE EDITOR'S FUNCTIONS 86

AUDIO..89
AUDIO CLIP INFORMATION...89
AUDIO CHANNELS..89
AUDIO TRACK CHANNELS 89
DISPLAY OPTIONS (FOR AUDIO CHANNELS) 90
CHANGE AUDIO TRACK CHANNELS 90
CONVERT STEREO TO MONO...90
DISPLAY OPTIONS (FOR AUDIO TRACKS) 90
RENAME AN AUDIO TRACK 91
AUDIO TRACK COLOR...91
SHOW AUDIO WAVEFORM (IN SOURCE VIEWER).................................91
ADJUST VOLUME..92
KEYFRAME VOLUME LINE 92
FADE AUDIO IN / OUT 93
PANNING...94
ADD VIDEO ONLY 94
ADD AUDIO ONLY...94
DELETE AUDIO FROM A VIDEO 95
AUDIO MIXER...95
AUDIO METERS..95
SYNCHRONIZE AUDIO 96
REVEAL A SYNCED AUDIO CLIP 96
RELINK MISSING AUDIO FILES 97
NUDGE AN AUDIO CLIP 97
SUBFRAME AUDIO EDITING 98
ADD AN AUDIO EFFECT 99
FULL AUDIO CONTROLS PANEL 99

Contents

DEACTIVATE AN AUDIO EFFECT 100

REMOVE AN AUDIO EFFECT 100

NOISE REDUCTION 100

EQUALIZER 102

NORMALIZE AUDIO 102

AUDIO COMPRESSOR 103

AUDIO COMPRESSOR (FAIRLIGHT) 104

FOLEY EFFECTS LIBRARY 105

EXPORT 106

EXPORT A SELECTION 106

QUICK EXPORT 107

DATA RATES 108

CHAPTER MARKERS 109

ALPHA CHANNEL 110

CUSTOM EXPORT SETTINGS 110

RENDERING (CACHING) 111

RENDER FORMATS 111

RENDER FILES FOLDER LOCATION 112

RENDERING MAY NOT BE NECESSARY 112

AUTOMATIC BACKGROUND RENDERING 113

RENDER PROGRESS BAR 113

RENDER IN PLACE 113

MANUAL RENDERING 114

EXPORT USING RENDER FILES 114

DELETE RENDER FILES 114

SETTINGS 116

2 KINDS OF SETTINGS IN DAVINCI RESOLVE 116

LIVE SAVE (AUTO SAVE) 116

SPECIFIC SETTINGS 117

CUSTOM SETTINGS 117

IMPROVE PERFORMANCE 118

AUTO PERFORMANCE MODE 118

STATUS DISPLAY 118

TIMELINE PROXY RESOLUTION 119

TIMELINE RESOLUTION 119

EXTERNAL VIDEO MONITOR 121

DISABLE EXTRA TIMELINES 121

BYPASS COLOR / FUSION EFFECTS 121

USE ADJUSTMENT CLIPS 121

USE COMPOUND CLIPS 122

MINIMIZE INTERFACE UPDATES 122

HIDE INTERFACE OVERLAYS 122

MEDIA MANAGEMENT 123

DATABASES 123

ENCODE 123

TRANSCODE 124

OFFLINE EDITING 124

Contents

ONLINE EDITING 124

MISSING MEDIA 125

RESOLUTION INDEPENDENCE...125

CODEC 125

FORMAT..126

ALPHA CHANNEL..127

MEDIA PREPARATION 127

PLUGIN MANAGEMENT 128

MEDIA MANAGEMENT COMMAND..128

CLIP ATTRIBUTES 129

INSPECTOR > FILE...129

INSPECTOR > IMAGE..129

RELINK MISSING MEDIA FILES..129

COPY TIMELINE TO A SECOND COMPUTER...............................130

OPTIMIZED MEDIA..131

PROXY MEDIA 132

VFX CONNECT 133

ARCHIVE A PROJECT 133

———

PREFACE

———

DaVinci Resolve Editing Step-By-Step Instructions was written to make the amazing features of DaVinci Resolve's *Edit Workspace* easy to use. It was written to give the filmmakers of today a straightforward book of step-by-step instructions for using DaVinci Resolve's editing procedures, transitions, titles, keyframes, visual effects, audio effects, export settings, media management preferences, performance enhancement techniques, and a host of other professional editing capabilities. Pro Tips with alternative work-a-rounds, adjustment layers, and keyboard shortcuts are included, and a comprehensive Table of Contents is added for easy access and easy navigation. *DaVinci Resolve Editing Step-By-Step Instructions* can be read as a full course of editing procedures for professional filmmakers or else it can be used as a basic book of step-by-step instructions for beginning filmmakers who simply want to edit their videos step-by-step.

———

INTRODUCTION

As the latest professional non-linear video editing software program (NLE) on the market – after Avid's *Media Composer*, Apple's *Final Cut Pro*, and Adobe's *Premiere Pro* – DaVinci Resolve's *Edit Workspace* has become one of the most widely antici-pated and widely respected NLEs today. It includes the same professional editing features of the other video editing programs, but it streamlines its features in a way that makes DaVinci Resolve extremely easy to use and extremely easy to under-stand. It eliminates the complicated folder structures found in the other NLEs, and it brings the good stuff up front so that its features and functions can be easily ac-cessed, easily appreciated, and easily applied.

DaVinci Resolve is a free professional video editing software program. (A paid ver-sion of DaVinci Resolve called *DaVinci Resolve Studio* – costing $295 – contains advanced "studio" features such as RAW video import and online collaboration. However, most filmmakers do not really shoot RAW video and most filmmakers do not really need online collaboration. As a result, the free version of DaVinci Resolve is essentially complete – and in fact remarkable – on its own. The free ver-sion of DaVinci Resolve has the same basic features of Avid, Final Cut Pro, and Premiere Pro, but without the expensive price tag.) DaVinci Resolve is a cross-platform NLE available for Mac, PC, and Linux users. There is even a DaVinci Re-solve editing app available for the iPad. DaVinci Resolve's Color Workspace, the industry standard for color grading, is included for free. DaVinci Resolve's motion graphics and special effects workspace Fusion is included for free. And DaVinci Resolve's DAW (digital audio workstation) Fairlight is included for free. DaVinci Resolve's amazing features and its state-of-the-art user-interface make DaVinci Resolve the most practical, the most pleasurable, and the most well-engineered video editing software program available today. It is very likely to become the premiere video editing software program of the future.

USER INTERFACE

The user interface of DaVinci Resolve's *Edit Workspace* is divided into 3 sections: the Source Viewer, the Timeline Viewer, and the Timeline. On the left side of the Source Viewer are the Media Pool and the Effects panels. The Media Pool and the Effects panels can be accessed by clicking the words *Media Pool* or *Effects* near the Source Viewer. On the right side of the Timeline Viewer are the Inspector and the Audio Mixer panels. The Inspector and the Audio Mixer panels can be accessed by clicking the words *Inspector* or *Mixer* near the Timeline Viewer. All of the panels in the DaVinci Resolve *Edit Workspace* can be activated or deactivated (i.e., shown or hidden) by clicking the name of each panel. A white panel's name indicates that it is activated (i.e., shown) and a gray panel's name indicates that it is deactivated (i.e., hidden). All of the panels in the DaVinci Resolve *Edit Workspace* can be re-sized and reshaped by dragging the edges of a panel in any direction.

Please Note: *DaVinci Resolve Editing Step-By-Step Instructions* uses two power keys from the Macintosh keyboard in some of its step-by-step instructions: Command and Option. PC users can use the Control and Alt power keys on the PC keyboard instead. Below are the two power keys (and the right-clicking function) from the Macintosh keyboard used in *DaVinci Resolve Editing Step-By-Step Instructions* and their PC counterparts.

- Command (Mac) = Control (PC).
- Option (Mac) = Alt (PC).
- Control-Click (Mac) = Right-Click (PC).

DaVinci Resolve's User Interface

VIEW

CLIP INFORMATION (METADATA)
You can see a video or audio clip's information (metadata) in DaVinci Resolve this way (Figure 01).
1. Select a video clip in the Media Pool or Timeline.
2. Inspector > File tab
    - Resolution, Frame Rate, Codec, Audio Codec, Audio Sample Rate/ Bit Depth, Duration, etc., are listed here.
        - There may be times when you need to see what codec, frame rate, or sample rate a particular video or audio clip has – for resizing, editing, or mixing, etc. – and a video or audio clip's technical information can be found here.

Figure 01: Clip Information

Figure 02: Activate Parameters

SHOW / HIDE PANELS
You can show or hide (i.e., activate or deactivate) panels in DaVinci Resolve this way.
- Click a panel's *name* (such as *Media Pool, Effects, Inspector, Mixer*, etc.) to activate or deactivate the panel.

- A white panel name = activated (visible).
- A gray panel name = deactivated (hidden).

ACTIVATE / DEACTIVATE PARAMETERS
You can activate or deactivate parameters in the Inspector in DaVinci Resolve this way (Figure 02).
1. Select a video or audio clip in a Timeline.
2. Inspector > Video (or Audio) > Click the red dot before a parameter listed.
   - Red dot = activated (visible).
   - Gray dot = deactivated (hidden).

MAXIMIZE SCREEN REAL ESTATE
You can maximize the screen real estate of DaVinci Resolve this way.
- Show or hide panels.
   - Click a panel's name.
- Resize panels.
   - Drag a panel's edge. (All panels resize this way.)

RED FOCUS LINE
You can have a red focus line appear above a selected panel in DaVinci Resolve to indicate that it is in operation this way.
- DaVinci Resolve Menu > Preferences > User > UI Settings > Click the Show Focus Indicators in the User Interface checkbox on.

FULL SCREEN VIEW
You can enter the different full screen views in DaVinci Resolve this way (Figure 03).
- Command F (Cinema Viewer)
   - or Workspace Menu > Viewer Mode > Cinema Viewer
- Option F (Enhanced Viewer)
   - or Workspace Menu > Viewer Mode > Enhanced Viewer
- Shift F (Full Page Viewer)
   - or Workspace Menu > Viewer Mode > Full Page Viewer

Figure 03: Full Screen View

Figure 04: Bypass Effects

BYPASS EFFECTS
You can bypass Fusion Effects (or Color Grades) applied to a video clip so that they will not appear in the Timeline Viewer in DaVinci Resolve this way (Figure 04).

- Click the Bypass icon located at the top of the Timeline Viewer.
  - or Shift D

BEFORE / AFTER VIEWS
You can show *before* and *after* views of a Fusion Effect (or a Color Grade) applied to a video clip in the Timeline Viewer to get a clearer view of what it looks like in DaVinci Resolve this way.

- Click the Bypass icon located at the top of the Timeline Viewer.
  - or Shift D

Figure 05: Broadcast Safe Area

Figure 06: Grid

BROADCAST SAFE AREAS
You can show the broadcast safe areas in the Timeline Viewer in DaVinci Resolve here (Figure 05).

- View Menu > Safe Area > On > Extents, Action, Title, Center (Cross Hair), or Aspect.
  - Pro Tip: You can add a grid or a Rule of Thirds grid on top of the Timeline Viewer to position your video clips or graphics files on a straight line or in a consistent manner this way (Figure 06).
    1. Add an Adjustment Clip to a Timeline.
       - Effects > Toolbox > Effects > Drag an Adjustment Clip to a layer above the other video clips in a Time-line.
    2. Add a grid to the Adjustment Clip.
       - Effects > Open FX > Drag the Grid Effect on top of the Adjustment Clip in the Timeline.

3. Inspector > Effects > Grid > Adjust the parameters of the Grid Effect.
4. Add this Adjustment Clip to a Power Bin in the Media Pool for reuse in all future projects, if you want.
   - Drag the Adjustment Clip to a Power Bin in the Media Pool. (Please see the *Power Bins* section of the *Media Pool* chapter in *Da Vinci Resolve Editing Step By Step Instructions* for an explanation of how to set up a Power Bin.)

DUAL MONITORS
You can set up dual monitors in DaVinci Resolve this way.
1. First, set up your computer to display dual monitors.
2. Workspace Menu > Dual Screen > On
   - Workspace Menu > Dual Screen > Full Screen Timeline

———

NAVIGATE

WORKSPACES
You can switch to DaVinci Resolve's seven different workspaces this way (Figure 07).
- Click a workspace icon at the bottom of the DaVinci Resolve user interface (Media, Cut, Edit, Color, Fusion, Fairlight, and Deliver).
    - or Workspace Menu > Switch to Page > Media, Cut, Edit, Color, Fusion, Fairlight, or Deliver (Figure 08).

 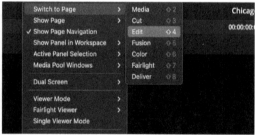

Figure 07: Workspaces   Figure 08: Workspaces Menu

WORKSPACE NAVIGATION TOOLBAR
You can show or hide the workspace navigation toolbar at the bottom of the DaVinci Resolve user interface here.
- Workspace Menu > Show Page Navigation

WORKSPACE NAVIGATION TEXT LABELS
You can show or hide the workspace navigation icon's text labels at the bottom of the DaVinci Resolve user interface here.

- Right click the workspace navigation toolbar at the bottom of DaVinci Resolve > Show Icons and Labels

RIGHT–CLICKING

Right-clicking items throughout DaVinci Resolve – to get a contextual menu (or a pop up menu) to appear – is one of the best ways to operate DaVinci Resolve. In fact, additional functions may appear on some of the contextual menus of DaVinci Resolve that are not always available in the drop down menus at the top of the DaVinci Resolve user interface.

KEYBOARD SHORTCUTS

DaVinci Resolve's keyboard shortcuts can be found, customized, and created here (Figure 09).

- DaVinci Resolve Menu > Keyboard Customization.

Figure 09: Keyboard Shortcuts   Figure 10: History Window

HISTORY WINDOW

DaVinci Resolve's History Window lists the stages of your previous work. It allows you to quickly move back to a previous stage of your work by simply clicking a stage listed in chronological order in the History Window.

- Edit Menu > History > Open History Window (Figure 10)

MEDIA POOL

————

DaVinci Resolve's Media Pool is where all media assets – video clips, audio clips, and/or graphics files – are imported and stored.

SHOW / HIDE MEDIA POOL
You can show or hide the Media Pool in DaVinci Resolve by clicking the words *Media Pool* at the top left corner of the Edit, Cut, or Media workspaces. If the Media Pool is grayed-out, it is deactivated (i.e., hidden). If the Media Pool is white, it is activated (i.e., visible).

VIEW OPTIONS
You can set up different view options in the Media Pool in DaVinci Resolve here.
  • Media Pool > Metadata View, Thumbnail View (Figure 11), List View

Figure 11: Thumbnail View   Figure 12: Sort by Clip Name

DISPLAY MEDIA ASSETS IN ORDER
You can have the Cut Workspace in DaVinci Resolve sort media assets in alphabetical order this way.

- Cut Workspace > Media Pool > Sort > Clip Name (Figure 12)
  - Pro Tip: Before import, if you renamed your video clips in a folder using the Finder's Batch Rename feature on a Mac, or renamed your video clips manually, they will appear listed in alphabetical order in the Media Pool for easy access.

EDIT INDEX

The Edit Index (near the Media Pool in DaVinci Resolve) lists all the clips, markers, flags, and edit points on video clips that have been placed into a Timeline. It looks like an Edit Decision List (EDL) of all edits that have been made, in technical terms. You can open (and even customize) the Edit Index in DaVinci Resolve this way.

1. Click the words *Edit Index* (near the words *Media Pool*) at the top of the DaVinci Resolve user interface.
   - Name, Duration, Codec, FPS, Color, Markers, Flags, Comments, etc., are arranged as columns of information in the Edit Index (Figure 13).
     - Pro Tip: You can customize the Edit Index to show only the columns of information that you want.
       - Select the Edit Index's . . . (Options) drop down menu.
     - Pro Tip: You can drag the columns of information to different positions and resize them individually for further customization.

IMPORT MEDIA

You can import media into DaVinci Resolve's Media Pool in several different ways. DaVinci Resolve's Edit, Cut, and Media workspaces all allow importing.
- Edit workspace > File Menu > Import > Media (Figure 14)
- Edit workspace > Media Pool > Right click a blank area in the Media Pool > Import Media
- Drag video clips, audio clips, and/or graphics files from a Finder window on a Mac and drop them directly into the Media Pool.

Figure 13: Edit Index

Figure 14: Import Media

BINS
Bins in DaVinci Resolve's Media Pool are "folders" that contain video clips, audio clips, and/or graphics files. They allow you to neatly organized your different media assets in different bins for easy access.

3 KINDS OF BINS
There are 3 kinds of bins in DaVinci Resolve's Media Pool.
1. Bins = folders containing media assets.
2. Smart Bins = folders automatically populated from asset metadata.
3. Power Bins = folders containing media assets available for reuse in all projects.

ADD A BIN
You can add a bin in DaVinci Resolve's Media Pool this way.
- Right-click a blank area below the *Master* area listed on the left side of the Media Pool > New Bin

RENAME A BIN
You can rename a bin in DaVinci Resolve's Media Pool this way.
- Right-click a bin > Rename Bin

CHANGE A BIN'S COLOR
You can color code a bin in DaVinci Resolve's Media Pool this way.
- Right-click a bin > Color Tag

SEPARATE BIN WINDOW
You can open up a Bin in the Media Pool in a separate window in DaVinci Resolve this way.
- Right-click a Bin > Open As New Window
    - Pro Tip: A separate bin can be dragged onto a second monitor if dual monitors have been set up.
    - Pro Tip: You can open up as many bins as separate windows as you want.

POWER BINS
Power Bins in DaVinci Resolve's Media Pool are folders that contain *reusable* media which can be used in all projects. You can put reusable items in your Power Bins such as music files, SFX files, titles, graphics files, textures, backgrounds, adjustment clips, grids, and just about anything else that you might want to reuse. You can create a Power Bin in DaVinci Resolve's Media Pool this way.

1. Click inside the Media Pool to make sure that the Media Pool is selected.
2. Media Pool > Master > . . . (Options) drop down menu > Show Power Bins (Figure 15)
3. Media Pool > Master > Power Bins > Right-click a blank area in the Power Bins area > New Bin (Figure 16)
4. Drag any item (title, graphics file, music file, adjustment clip, etc.) from the Media Pool or a Timeline into a Power Bin for reuse in other projects.

Figure 15: Power Bins   Figure 16: New Bin

SOURCE VIEWER

———

The Source Viewer in DaVinci Resolve is a video screen that plays videos from the Media Pool. While a video is playing, you can add *in* and *out* points to a section of the video and then drag just the section of the video to a Timeline. (See *In and Out Points* explained below.)

PREVIEW A VIDEO CLIP
You can preview a video clip in the Source Viewer in DaVinci Resolve this way.
- Skim (i.e., scrub) a video clip in the Media Pool by hovering and moving your mouse cursor over it (Figure 17).
  - Enlarge the video clip thumbnails in the Media Pool by dragging the resize slider at the top, if needed.

Figure 17: Scrub   Figure 18: Single/Double Viewer

OPEN A VIDEO CLIP
You can open up a video clip directly in the Source Viewer in DaVinci Resolve this way.
- Double-click a video clip in the Media Pool.

PLAY / PAUSE A VIDEO CLIP

You can play and pause a video clip in the Source Viewer in DaVinci Resolve this way.

1. Click the Source Viewer's screen to make sure that the Source Viewer is selected.
2. Press the space bar once (for play) and press the space bar again (for pause).
   - Pro Tip: Pressing the space bar on or off (to play and pause a video) is a very efficient way of operating all of the workspaces in DaVinci Resolve.

SHOW A VIDEO CLIP FROM A TIMELINE

You can show a video clip from a Timeline in the Source Viewer in DaVinci Resolve this way.

1. Select a video clip in a Timeline.
2. Press F.
   - The video clip will appear in the Source Viewer in its entirety, with its original *in* and *out* points included.

SINGLE VIEWER MODE

The Single Viewer Mode in DaVinci Resolve displays one viewer screen, not two, at the top of the user interface. Normally, two viewer screens are displayed: the Source Viewer and the Timeline Viewer. But in Single Viewer Mode, only one screen appears. Both the source video clips from the Media Pool and the video clips from the Timeline play interchangeably inside this one screen during Single Viewer Mode. You can use the Single Viewer Mode in DaVinci Resolve this way.

- Click the Single Viewer Mode icon (the small single window icon) at the top of the Timeline Viewer (Figure 18).
  - or Workspace Menu > Single Viewer Mode
- You can return to using both viewer screens (default) by clicking the Single Viewer Mode icon again at the top of the Timeline Viewer.
  - or Workspace Menu > Select the Single Viewer Mode again.

IN / OUT POINTS

You can add *in* and *out* points to a section of a video clip in the Source Viewer and then drag the section of the video to a Timeline in DaVinci Resolve this way. This is a preferred way of adding video clips to a Timeline over adding entire video clips, because entire video clips will need to be resized later.

1. Double click a video clip in the Media Pool to open it up in the Source Viewer.

2. Play the video clip by pressing the spacebar (play) and pressing the spacebar again (pause) whenever needed.

3. Press the letter I to create an *in* point at the start of a section of the video clip that you want. The *in* point will be created underneath the playhead (Figure 19).

4. Press the letter O to create an *out* point at the end of the section of the video clip that you want. The *out* point will be created underneath the playhead.

   • Pro Tip: You can resize the section of a video clip in the Source Viewer at any time by simply dragging the *in* and *out* points that appear at the bottom of the Source Viewer.

   • Pro Tip: You can remove your *in* and *out* points and start all over again if you have made a mistake by pressing Option X (Figure 20).

   • Pro Tip: You can navigate a video clip in the Source Viewer by pressing the J, K, and L keys on the keyboard. J is rewind. K is stop. L is forward. Pressing J repeatedly is fast rewind. Pressing L repeatedly is fast forward. As usual, you can add *in* and *out* points to any section of a video clip that you like by pressing the I and the O keys on the keyboard while playing (or stopping) the video. (Please note: while the J, K, and L keys may be difficult to navigate at first for beginning video editors, the J, K, and L keys can come in extremely handy when a lot of video clips need sorting in a speedy way. (J, K, and L keys are explained further in the *Editing* chapter of *DaVinci Resolve Editing Step By Step Instructions*.)

5. Drag this section of the video clip (between its *in* and *out* points) from the Source Viewer to a Timeline.

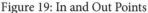

Figure 19: In and Out Points

Figure 20: Delete In and Out Points (Option X)

TIMELINE

MULTIPLE TIMELINES

Multiple Timelines can be used in DaVinci Resolve for creating different versions of a video, for collaborating with others editors, for creating different sections of a longer film and splicing the sections together later when the film is complete, or for improving the performance of DaVinci Resolve since smaller timelines process more efficiently than longer timelines. You can create multiple timelines in DaVinci Resolve, if you want, this way.

1. Right-click a blank area in the Media Pool > Timelines > Create New Timeline (Figure 21)
2. Add video clips to the newly created Timeline.
3. Switch between multiple Timelines by selecting the different Timelines listed in the Timelines drop down menu at the top of the Timeline Viewer (Figure 22).

Figure 21: Create New Timeline

Figure 22: Timelines List

CREATE A TIMELINE

You can create a Timeline in DaVinci Resolve this way.

- File Menu > New Timeline

- A file for the Timeline (called Timeline1) is added to the Media Pool.
- Please Note: A Timeline is automatically created when you drag a video clip from the Media Pool into a Timeline for the first time.

DUPLICATE A TIMELINE

You can work on copies (duplicates) of a Timeline to experiment with different editing approaches on and not lose work done on an original Timeline. You can duplicate a Timeline in DaVinci Resolve this way.

- Right-click a Timeline in the Media Pool > Duplicate Timeline
  - or Select a Timeline in the Media Pool > Edit Menu > Duplicate Timeline (Figure 23)

Figure 23: Duplicate a Timeline   Figure 24: Timeline Zoom Slider

ZOOM

You can zoom in and out of a Timeline in DaVinci Resolve in several different ways.

1. Timeline Toolbar > Zoom Slider (Figure 24)
   - Drag the Zoom Slider's center dot or click anywhere on the Zoom Slider.
     - The Timeline will zoom in or out directly underneath the playhead, so you may want to position the playhead first before zooming.
2. Timeline Toolbar > Zoom Slider
   - Click the + (plus) or - (minus) icons at the ends of the Zoom Slider.
3. Keyboard Shortcuts:
   - Select the Timeline first by clicking on a blank area inside the Timeline.
     - Command + = zoom in.
     - Command - = zoom out.

ZOOM TO FIT

You can have all video clips in a Timeline fit inside its viewable area in DaVinci Resolve this way.

1. Select the Timeline first by clicking on a blank area inside the Timeline.
2. Shift Z
   - or Click the Full Extent Zoom icon in the Timeline Toolbar.

Figure 25: Half Screen (Shrink) icon – Left   Figure 26: Half Screen (Shrink) icon – Right

FULL–WIDTH TIMELINE

You can increase the viewable area of a Timeline in DaVinci Resolve this way.

1. Close the Media Pool (or Effects Panel) half way on the left side of the DaVinci Resolve user interface. When closed half way, the Timeline will be unobstructed.
   - Click the Half Screen (Shrink) icon located at the top of the Media Pool or Effects Panel (Figure 25).
     - Click it again to re-extend the Media Pool or Effects Panel to full length.
2. Close the Inspector half way on the right side of the DaVinci Resolve user interface. When closed half way, the Timeline will be unobstructed.
   - Click the Half Screen (Shrink) icon located at the top of the Inspector (Figure 26).
     - Click it again to re-extend the Inspector to full length.

BIG TIMECODE WINDOW

- Workspace Menu > Timecode Window
  - This Timecode Window can be resized and moved anywhere.

PLAYBACK POST ROLL

Playback Post Roll allows the playhead in DaVinci Resolve's Timeline to continue playing after the last clip, when it normally stops (by default) at the end of the last clip.

- Timeline > Playback Post-Roll (Figure 27)

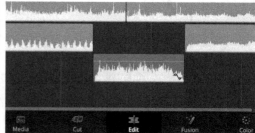

Figure 27: Playback Post-Roll   Figure 28: Timeline Scroll Bar

SCROLL

You can scroll the Timeline in DaVinci Resolve this way.
- Drag the center portion of the horizontal scroll bar at the bottom of the Timeline in DaVinci Resolve (Figure 28).

MOVE PLAYHEAD TO START OF VIDEO CLIP

You can move the playhead to the start of a video clip in a Timeline in DaVinci Resolve this way.
1. Position the playhead on a video clip.
2. Press the Up Arrow key.
    - The playhead will move to the start of the video clip.

MOVE PLAYHEAD TO END OF VIDEO CLIP

You can move the playhead to the end of a video clip in a Timeline in DaVinci Resolve this way.
1. Position the playhead on a video clip.
2. Press the Down Arrow key.
    - The playhead will move to the end of the video clip.

SELECT ALL VIDEO CLIPS AFTER PLAYHEAD

You can select all video clips under and after the playhead in a Timeline in DaVinci Resolve this way.
1. Position the playhead on a video clip.
2. Press Y.
    - This can be useful when you want to manually place a video clip in the middle of a Timeline, in between clips, and you don't want to overwrite any other neighboring video clips. You can first move the other clips out of the way.
        A. Position the playhead on a video clip.
        B. Press Y.

- All the video clips after the playhead will be selected.
  C. Drag the selected video clips after the playhead downstream (i.e., down the Timeline).
  D. Drag a video clip from the Media Pool into the Timeline.
  E. Drag the selected video clips downstream on the Timeline back upstream to their original position.
    - Make sure Snapping is turned on.

SELECT ALL VIDEO CLIPS BEFORE PLAYHEAD
You can select all video clips under and before the playhead in a Timeline in DaVinci Resolve this way.
1. Position the playhead on a video clip.
2. Press Command Y.

NUDGE PLAYHEAD
You can nudge the playhead in a Timeline in DaVinci Resolve this way.
- Left Arrow key = nudges the playhead left one frame.
- Right Arrow key = nudges the playhead right one frame.

NUDGE A VIDEO CLIP
You can nudge a video clip in a Timeline in DaVinci Resolve this way.
- Select a video clip in a Timeline first.
  - Comma = nudges a video clip left one frame.
  - Period = nudges a video clip right one frame.
    - Pro Tip: Nudging the playhead, a video clip, or even an edit point in DaVinci Resolve can be a very effective way of precisely refining your edit decisions.

PLAY AROUND A SELECTION
You can have the playhead in DaVinci Resolve play around a small area in a Timeline to see an editing adjustment more clearly.
1. Position the playhead over a video clip in a Timeline.
2. Press / Forward Slash
   - or Playback > Play Around / To

UNDO / REDO
You can undo (and redo) all actions created in DaVinci Resolve this way.
- Command Z = undo.
- Command Shift Z = redo.

DISPLAY OPTIONS (FOR VIDEO CLIPS)

You can configure DaVinci Resolve's Timeline to display video clips in 3 different ways.

- Click the Timeline View Options icon at the far left side of the Timeline Toolbar > Video View Options (Figure 29) >
    1. Film Strip View = all the frames of a video clip are displayed.
    2. Thumbnail View = only the frames at the start and end of a video clip are displayed (as thumbnails). The middle frames are left blank.
    3. Simple View = plain rectangles of a video clip (with no frames at all) are displayed.

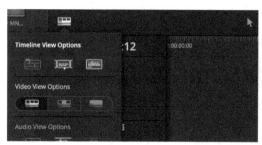

Figure 29: Video View Options

Figure 30: Clip Color

CHANGE A VIDEO CLIP'S COLOR

You can change a video clip's color in DaVinci Resolve this way.

- Right-click a video clip (or an audio clip) in a Timeline > Clip Color (Figure 30)

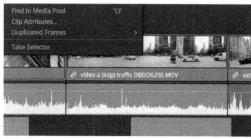

Figure 31: Find in Media Pool

Figure 32: Reveal in Finder

LOCATE A VIDEO CLIP FROM TIMELINE

You can find a video clip that was placed in a Timeline in DaVinci Resolve this way.

1. DaVinci Resolve Menu > Preferences > User > Editing > Click the Always Highlight Current Clip in the Media Pool checkbox on.
2. Select a video or audio clip in a Timeline.
   - It will appear highlighted in the Media Pool
     - Pro Tip: You can also locate a video clip from a Timeline in the Finder in a computer this way.
       A. Right click a video clip in a Timeline > Find in Media Pool (Figure 31)
       B. Right click the video clip in the Media Pool > Reveal in Finder (Figure 32)

SHOW USED VIDEO CLIPS

You can see which video clips in the Media Pool are used in a Timeline in DaVinci Resolve this way.
- A red line appears on all video clips in the Media Pool that have been placed in a Timeline.
  - This is helpful because it lets you see which video clips from the Media Pool have been placed in a Timeline and which video clips have not.

MARKER

You can add a marker to a video clip in a Timeline in DaVinci Resolve this way.
1. Position the playhead over a video clip in a Timeline where you want to add a marker.
2. Press M
   - or Click the Marker icon in the Timeline Toolbar.
     - Pro Tip: Markers can be dragged to new positions once they have been placed, their colors can be changed for easier recognition, and they can be deleted. Notes (or annotations) can also be added to Markers.
       - Select a Marker > Mark Menu > Modify Marker

FLAG

You can add a flag to a video clip in a Timeline in DaVinci Resolve this way.
1. Position the playhead over a video clip in a Timeline where you want to add a flag.
2. Click the Flag icon in the Timeline's Toolbar.
   - Please Note: Flags "flag" a whole video clip whereas markers "mark" a specific frame of a video clip.

DEACTIVATE A VIDEO CLIP

Deactivating a video clip temporarily deactivates (turns off) a video clip in a Timeline. It makes the video clip go dim, and it will not show up during playback or export. You can deactivate a video clip in DaVinci Resolve this way.

1. Select a video clip in a Timeline.
2. Press D (Figure 33).
3. Reactivate the video clip again.
    *   Press D again.
        *   Pro Tip: Deactivating a video clip in DaVinci Resolve's Timeline can be very useful when auditioning different video clips that you might want to include in a scene. You can place 4 video clips above each other (on different tracks) in a Timeline, for example, and deactivate and activate them one by one in order to audition which one works best. You can deactivate and activate audio clips in the same way.

Figure 33: Deactivate a Clip

Figure 34: Add a Gap (Adjustment Clip)

DELETE A VIDEO CLIP

You can delete a video clip in a Timeline in DaVinci Resolve this way.

1. Select a video clip in a Timeline.
2. Press Delete.

CREATE A GAP

You can add a gap between video clips in a Timeline in DaVinci Resolve this way.

1. Effects > Toolbox > Effects > Drag an Adjustment Clip to a Timeline.
2. Resize the Adjustment Clip by dragging its ends (Figure 34).
3. Drag the Adjustment Clip to wherever you want in the Timeline.
    *   An Adjustment Clip is a blank video clip that will not show up on export (unless you add something to it, such as an effect, when it is above another video clip).

FOCUS SELECT A VIDEO CLIP

You can focus select a video clip in a Timeline in DaVinci Resolve this way.

1. Position the playhead over a video clip in a Timeline.
2. Press X.
   - The video clip underneath the playhead in the Timeline will be selected. This means that you can now quickly apply effects or actions of any kind to the entire length of the video clip.

FADE IN / OUT

You can have a video clip in a Timeline in DaVinci Resolve fade in or out this way.

1. Hover the mouse cursor over the top edge of a video clip (or an audio clip) in a Timeline.
2. Drag the white boxes that appear in the top right and left corners inward.
   - A Tool Tip shows the number of frames the fade in or out uses so that you can create a long fade or a short fade.

DISPLAY OPTIONS (FOR TRACKS)

You can configure DaVinci Resolve's Timeline to display video tracks in 3 different ways.

- Select the Timeline View Options icon at the left side of the Timeline Toolbar > Timeline View Options (Figure 35) >
  1. Stacked Timelines = stacked timelines are displayed on different tracks. Multiple timelines can be displayed.
  2. Subtitle Tracks = subtitles are displayed.
  3. Audio Waveforms = audio waveforms of the audio portion of video clips are displayed.

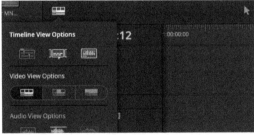
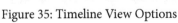

Figure 35: Timeline View Options

Figure 36: Track Height Slider

TRACK HEIGHT

You can configure DaVinci Resolve's Timeline to display a track's height in different ways.

- Timeline View Options > Drag the Track Height (Video or Audio) slider (Figure 36).
  - or Drag a track header's top dividing line up or down.

INCREASE AUDIO TRACKS AREA
You can increase the viewable area of the audio tracks in a Timeline in DaVinci Resolve this way.
- Drag the dividing line between the audio tracks and the video tracks in a Timeline up.

CHANGE A TRACK'S COLOR
You can change a track's color in DaVinci Resolve this way.
- Right-click a track header in a Timeline > Change Track Color

ADD A NEW TRACK
You can add a new track in DaVinci Resolve this way.
- Right-click a track header in a Timeline > Add Track

DELETE A TRACK
You can delete a track in DaVinci Resolve this way.
- Right-click a track header in a Timeline > Delete Track

RENAME A TRACK
You can rename a track in DaVinci Resolve this way.
- Click a track header's name in a Timeline > Type a new name.

MOVE A TRACK UP / DOWN
You can move a track up or down in DaVinci Resolve this way.
- Right-click a track header in a Timeline > Move Track Up or Move Track Down

LOCK A TRACK
You can lock a track in DaVinci Resolve this way.
- Click the Lock icon on a track header in a Timeline.

———

EDITING BASICS

ROUGH CUT
A *rough cut* in editing is typically made by a video editor during the first stage of the editing process. It involves adding video clips to a Timeline and arranging them in a *rough order*. It is a first assembly.

FINAL CUT
A *final cut* in editing is typically made by a video editor during the last stage of the editing process. It involves trimming the video clips in a Timeline so that they can play together well. It is the last assembly.

3 STEPS IN VIDEO EDITING
There are 3 steps involved in editing video clips.
1. *Add* video clips to a Timeline.
2. *Move* video clips (i.e., rearrange video clips) in a Timeline.
3. *Resize* video clips (i.e., trim video clips) in a Timeline.

ADD VIDEO CLIPS TO A TIMELINE
You can add video clips to a Timeline in DaVinci Resolve's Edit workspace in several different ways.
1. The simplest way to add video clips to a Timeline in DaVinci Resolve is to simply drag a video clip from the Media Pool into a Timeline. This will create a new Timeline automatically. The entire range of this video clip, however, will be added to the Timeline, and this means that it will have to be resized (or trimmed) eventually to fit in well with the other neighboring video clips around it.
2. A more effective, but more time-consuming way to add video clips to a Timeline in DaVinci Resolve's Edit workspace is to open up a video clip in

the Source Viewer first, add *in* and *out* points to it (so only a section of the video clip will be selected), and then drag the section of the video clip to the Timeline.

    A. Double click a video clip in the Media Pool so it will open up in the Source Viewer.

    B. Play the video clip in the Source Viewer.

    C. Add *in* and *out* points to the video clip while playing it.

        I. Press the letter I on the keyboard at the start of a section of the video clip that you like. This will add an *in* point underneath the playhead (Figure 37).

        II. Press the letter O on the keyboard at the end of a section of the video clip that you like. This will add an *out* point underneath the playhead.

          • The video clip's *in* and *out* points are represented by a line at the bottom of the Source Viewer.

             • Pro Tip: You can remove your *in* and *out* points and start all over again if you have made a mistake by pressing Option X.

    D. Drag this section of the video clip (between the *in* and *out* points) from the Source Viewer to the Timeline.

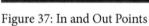

Figure 37: In and Out Points   Figure 38: Edit Overlays

3. The Edit Overlays in the Timeline Viewer in DaVinci Resolve is another way to add video clips to a Timeline (Figure 38).

    A. Double-click a video clip in the Media Pool to open it up in the Source Viewer.

    B. Drag the video clip from the Source Viewer's screen and hover it over the Timeline Viewer's screen.

        • Seven different Edit Overlays will appear on the Timeline Viewer's screen.

          • Insert

- Overwrite
- Replace
- Fit to Fill
- Place on Top
- Append at End
- Ripple Overwrite

C. Drop the video clip onto one of the Edit Overlays that appear on the Timeline Viewer's screen. The video clip will then enter the Timeline according to the Edit Overlay's specific instructions.

- *Insert* = inserts a video clip where the playhead is parked in a Timeline. The neighboring video clips will ripple (i.e., move) out of the way for the video clip to fit in.
- *Overwrite* = overwrites a video clip over the footage in the timeline where the playhead is parked.
- *Replace* = replaces a video clip in the Timeline where the playhead is parked.
- *Fit to Fill* = fits a video clip into an area of the Timeline that is blank.
- *Place on Top* = places a video clip on a track above the other video clips in the Timeline where the playhead is parked (as B-Roll).
- *Append* = adds a video clip to the *end* of the Timeline (*append* means add to the *end*).
- *Ripple Overwrite* = overwrites footage in the Timeline that the playhead is parked on and ripples (i.e., moves) the neighboring video clips out of the way to do so.
  - Note: using an Edit Overlay on a different track in a timeline (other than on track 1) requires you to first target that track by clicking the V2 or V3 item on its track header. A box around the V2 or V3 item on the track header indicates it is targeted. (f you are targeting a different track in the Timeline, please see *Target a Destination Track* explained below.)

4. Three-Point Editing is another way to add video clips to a Timeline. Three-Point Editing overwrites a video clip in a Timeline at the playhead and according to the *in* and *out* points that have been set in the Source Viewer. You can use Three-Point Editing in DaVinci Resolve this way.

A. Press I to set an *in* point on a video clip in the Source Viewer (this is point 1).

B. Press I and then press O to set *in* and *out* points on a video clip (or video clips) in a Timeline where you want the video clip from the Source Viewer to be inserted (these are points 2 and 3).

C. Drag the video clip from the Source Viewer above the Timeline Viewer and drop it onto the *Overwrite* Edit Overlay.

- Your video clip will overwrite the video clip (or video clips) in the Timeline between where you set *in* and *out* points, and it will start on the *in* point that was set on the video clip in the Source viewer.

5. Back-Timed Editing is another way to add video clips to a Timeline. Back-Timed Editing uses an *out* point on a video clip in the Source Viewer instead of an *in* point as in Three-Point Editing. Set both *in* and *out* points in the Source Viewer first. It then uses the same Three-Point Editing process described above in *Three-Point Editing*.

Figure 39: Video Track 2 (V2)

Figure 40: Y Selects All Clips After Playhead

DESTINATION TRACK

A track-based NLE such as DaVinci Resolve requires a video track in a Timeline to be targeted (i.e., selected) before any video clips from the Source Viewer can be added to it. This is not needed, of course, if you are just adding video clips to one track (since track 1 is targeted automatically in DaVinci Resolve during editing). You can target a "different" destination track in DaVinci Resolve, if needed, this way.

1. Click the V2 item on a track header in a Timeline (V2 means "Video Track 2") (Figure 39)

- A red box forms around the V2 item when its track is targeted. (No box around V2 means that the track is not targeted.)
- Remove a track's targeting by clicking its V2 item again.

- Please Note: Targeting a destination track is not needed when dragging and dropping video clips into a Timeline in DaVinci Resolve. It is only needed when using the Edit Overlays described above.
- Please Note As Well: When you drag a video clip from the Source Viewer to another track in a Timeline such as to track 2, track 3, or track 4, for example, a new track will be added automatically.

MOVE VIDEOS IN A TIMELINE

You can easily drag a video clip in a Timeline to a new location at any time.

1. Select the Select Tool or the Trim Tool in the Timeline Toolbar.
2. Drag a video clip in the Timeline to a new position.
   - Be careful not to overwrite any neighboring video clips in the process.
     - Pro Tip: If necessary, you can first move the neighboring video clips in a Timeline out of the way (or to a track above), drag a new video clip in, and then move the other video clips back in to avoid overwriting them.
       - Press Y to select all video clips after the playhead (or Press Command Y to select all video clips before the playhead) (Figure 40).
         - Snapping must be on for this to work.

SNAPPING

Snapping "snaps" a video clip's end to another video clip's end in a Timeline when it is moved. This prevents a video clip from overwriting another video clip when it is moved. It also prevents a moved video clip from leaving a gap in a Timeline. It allows a video clip to "snap" to the end of a nearby video clip and to playback therefore perfectly. You can turn Snapping on and off in DaVinci Resolve this way.

- Click the Snapping (magnet) icon in the Timeline Toolbar.
  - or Timeline Menu > Snapping (Figure 41)

Figure 41: Snapping

Figure 42: Slip Edit

SLIP EDIT

A Slip Edit "slips" a video clip in a Timeline underneath its two ends. Its ends stay the same, but the clip underneath moves. This can be extremely useful in precisely positioning a video clip underneath its edit points. You can Slip Edit a video clip in DaVinci Resolve this way.

1. Select the Trim Tool in the Timeline Toolbar.
2. Drag the *top half* of a video clip in a Timeline that you want to "slip" left or right (Figure 42).
    - The video clip inside its two ends moves, but its ends do not.

SLIDE EDIT

A Slide Edit "slides" a video clip in a Timeline left or right, including its two ends. It overwrites the neighboring video clips around it, and, as a result, it is almost never useful. You can Slide Edit a video clip in DaVinci Resolve this way.

1. Select the Select Tool in the Timeline Toolbar.
2. Drag the *bottom half* of a video clip in a Timeline left or right.
    - Be Aware: Since the ends of this video clip overwrite the ends of all neighboring video clips in a Timeline when moved, it can ruin the previous edits you have made.

COPY A VIDEO CLIP

You can copy a video clip in DaVinci Resolve this way.

- Hold Option while dragging a video clip in a Timeline. (Option-dragging creates a copy of an item automatically.)

DELETE A VIDEO CLIP

You can delete a video clip in DaVinci Resolve this way.

1. Select a video clip in a Timeline.
2. Press Delete.

MOVE A VIDEO CLIP TO A DIFFERENT TRACK

You can move a video clip to a different track – in a straight line – in DaVinci Resolve this way.

- Hold Shift while dragging a video clip up or down to a different track in a Timeline (Shift-drag it).
    - This is useful when you want to move a video clip up or down to a different track in a Timeline – in a straight line – and do not want to disrupt the arrangement of the other video clips you have worked on beforehand, or when you want to preserve a video clip's audio syncing.

ADD A GAP
You can add a gap to a Timeline in DaVinci Resolve this way.
1. Create an Adjustment Clip
    A. Effects > Toolbox > Effects > Drag an Adjustment Clip to a Timeline.
    B. Resize the Adjustment Clip by dragging its ends.
2. Drag the Adjustment Clip to wherever you want in the Timeline.
    • An Adjustment Clip is a blank video clip that will not show up in the Timeline Viewer or on export (unless you add something to it, such as an effect, when it is above another video clip).

3 RESIZING TOOLS
3 resizing tools are available in a Timeline in DaVinci Resolve.
1. Select Tool (A) = selects, moves, and trims video clips in a Timeline. It cannot be used to create Slip Edits.
2. Trim Tool (T) = selects, moves, and trims video clips in a Timeline just as the Select Tool, but it can also be used to creates Slip Edits. The Trim Tool has more functionality than the Select Tool in DaVinci Resolve.
3. Dynamic Trim Tool = makes scrubbing video clips in a Timeline extremely smooth and easy. It works in conjunction with the Select Tool or the Trim Tool, and it cannot work alone. It uses real-time playback.
    A. Select the Dynamic Trim Tool in the Timeline Toolbar.
    B. Select the Select Tool or the Trim Tool in the Timeline Toolbar to work in conjunction with the Dynamic Trim Tool.
        • You can now skim (i.e., scrub) by dragging the playhead over video clips in a Timeline smoothly and easily.

RESIZE VIDEO CLIPS
You can resize (i.e., trim) video clips in a Timeline in DaVinci Resolve this way.
1. Select either the Select Tool or the Trim Tool in the Timeline Toolbar.
2. Drag the end of a video clip.
    • The video clip resizes.
        • Pro Tip: You may have to zoom in first to see the end of a video clip more clearly before dragging it.
        • Please Note: Zooming in and out of a Timeline in DaVinci Resolve is a very important skill to learn because it improves an editor's ability to make edits quickly. It allows an editor to see an edit point more clearly, make a precise edit, and then zoom back out again to see an entire Timeline. You can zoom in and out of DaVinci Resolve's Timeline in several different ways.
            1. Timeline Toolbar > Zoom Slider

- Drag the center dot or click anywhere in the Zoom Slider.
2. Timeline Toolbar > Zoom Slider
   - Click the + (plus) or - (minus) icons at the ends of the Zoom Slider.
3. Keyboard Shortcuts:
   - Select the Timeline first by clicking on a blank area inside the Timeline.
     - Command + = zoom in.
     - Command - = zoom out.

ROLL EDIT

A Roll Edit "rolls" both the ends of a video clip and a neighboring video clip in a Timeline when a video clip is resized. If the end of a video clip is dragged outward to be lengthened, for example, it will shorten the neighboring video clip so that the overall length of the Timeline will remain the same. If the end of a video clip is dragged inward to be shortened, it will lengthen the neighboring video clip so that the overall length of the Timeline will remain the same. You can resize a video clip in a Timeline with a Roll Edit in DaVinci Resolve this way.

1. Select the Trim Tool in the Timeline Toolbar.
2. Drag the center point between 2 neighboring video clips in a Timeline (not the edge of one video clip) so that both ends are selected (Figure 43).
   - The adjoining video clips should have handles in order to work.
   - The 2-Up Display will automatically appear in the Timeline Viewer to help you see more closely how your edit changes look. It allows you to see where one video clip ends and where the next video clip begins.
   - A Tool Tip also appears by the mouse cursor while dragging, showing you the changes you make in seconds and frames.

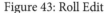

Figure 43: Roll Edit

Figure 44: Ripple Edit

RIPPLE EDIT

A Ripple Edit "ripples" (i.e., moves) the neighboring video clips in a Timeline downstream (or upstream) when a video clip is resized. If the end of a video clip is dragged outward it will push all neighboring videos clips downstream. If the end of a video clip is dragged inward it will pull all neighboring video clips upstream. You can resize a video clip in a Timeline with a Ripple Edit in DaVinci Resolve this way.

1. Select the Trim Tool in the Timeline Toolbar.
2. Drag the end of a video clip in a Timeline inward or outward (Figure 44).
   - The adjoining video clips should have handles in order to work.
   - The 2-Up Display will automatically appear in the Timeline Viewer to help you see more closely how your edit changes look. It allows you to see where one video clip ends and where the next video clip begins.
   - A Tool Tip also appears by the mouse cursor while dragging, showing you the changes you make in seconds and frames.

NUDGE EDIT POINT (2-UP DISPLAY)

You can nudge an edit point in DaVinci Resolve this way.

1. Select a video clip's edit point in a Timeline.
2. Use the following keyboard shortcuts:
   - Comma = moves the edit point left one frame.
   - Period = moves the edit point right one frame.
     - Pro Tip: You can nudge a video clip's edit point quickly by pressing the comma and/or the period keys on the keyboard repeatedly. You can also watch the 2-Up Display on the Timeline Viewer to see how your edit changes look (Figure 45).This can be helpful in precisely fine-tuning your edit points.

Figure 45: 2-Up Display

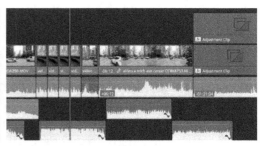

Figure 46: Top and Tail Edits

TOP / TAIL EDITS

Top and Tail Edits allow you to quickly trim a video clip's end according to where the playhead is parked over it. You can resize a video clip in a Timeline with a Top or Tail Edit in DaVinci Resolve this way.

1. Position the playhead over a video clip where you want to resize it (i.e., create a trim).
   A. Press Shift [(left bracket) to trim the video clip's start point (top) to where the playhead is located (Figure 46).
   B. Press Shift] (right bracket) to trim the video clip's end point (tail) to where the playhead is located.
      - Pro Tip: Top and Tail Edits can speed up your video trimming process significantly.

JKL EDITING

J, K, and L Editing allows you to quickly navigate the playhead over a video clip (or video clips) in a Timeline when you are looking for a good place to create an Edit Point. You simply press the J, K, and L keys on the keyboard to navigate backward, forward, and to stop. You can use the J, K, and L keys on the keyboard to navigate in DaVinci Resolve this way.

- J = rewind (reverse).
- K = stop.
- L = play (forward).
- J pressed repeatedly = fast rewind.
- L pressed repeatedly = fast forward.
- Holding K and tapping J = rewinds in slow-motion (one frame at a time).
- Holding K and tapping L = plays forward in slow-motion (one frame at a time).
   - Pro Tip: J, K, and L editing can come in extremely handy when you have a lot of video clips to sort and trim.
   - Pro Tip: J, K, and L editing can also be used while navigating video clips in the Media Pool or the Source Viewer, and not just in the Timeline.

SPLIT A VIDEO CLIP

You can resize a video clip in a Timeline by splitting it in DaVinci Resolve this way.

1. Select the Razor Blade Tool in the Timeline Toolbar.
2. Click anywhere on a video clip in a Timeline.
   - The video clip will be split in two.
      - Pro Tip: Splitting a video clip can also occur without using the Razor Blade Tool.

A. Position the playhead over a video clip where you want to create a split.
B. Hold down the Command key and press B (Command-click B).

COMPOUND CLIP

A Compound Clip in DaVinci Resolve can flatten multiple tracks of video clips into one track or preserve complicated edit points made on a series of video clips in a Timeline. This can help protect the video clips from being accidentally altered. You can create a Compound Clip in DaVinci Resolve this way.

1. Select a range of contiguous video clips (or tracks of video clips) in a Timeline (Figure 47).
2. Right-click one of the video clips > New Compound Clip (Figure 48)
3. Reopen a Compound Clip.
   - Right-click a Compound Clip > Decompose in Place > Using Clips Only

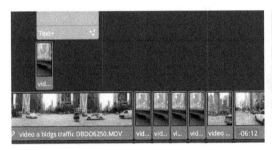 

Figure 47: Clip Layers   Figure 48: Compound Clip

PLAY AROUND AN EDIT POINT

Playing Around an Edit Point in a Timeline, after you have made an Edit Point, allows you to have a better view of how an Edit Point will look in playback. You can Play Around an Edit Point in a Timeline in DaVinci Resolve this way.

1. Position the playhead over an Edit Point that you have created in a Timeline
2. Press / Forward Slash
   - or Playback Menu > Play Around/To
   - Pro Tip: You can Press / Forward Slash repeatedly to get repeated views.

EDITING CONCEPTS

———

CONTINUITY EDITING

Continuity Editing (a.k.a. Invisible Editing) hides the editing splices (or cuts) between shots in a movie so that an audience will not be able to see them. It works by "cutting on action." The same action of an actor sitting down in a scene, for example, from one camera angle, spliced together with the actor sitting down from a different angle – with the same action – will not be seen. The two shots from the different camera angles fit together perfectly because they contain the same action. They can be spliced together where the action in both shots meet. Continuity Editing means that the action in shot A "continues" in shot B. The action in shot A "matches" the action in shot B. Continuity Editing (a.k.a. Invisible Editing) requires the director of a scene in a movie to get two shots of an actor performing the same action from two different camera angles. The actor will also be required to do the same action twice.

PARALLEL EDITING

Parallel Editing (also known as "cross-cutting") edits together two different perspectives of a situation in a movie in *parallel*. It provides an audience with a greater variety of perspectives to watch and it adds dramatic context. A perfect example of parallel editing is a chase scene in a movie. The shots of the person being chased are "cross-cut" (i.e., intercut in *parallel*) with the shots of the person giving the chase. The two shots contain different perspectives of the same situation in *parallel*. In fact, most feature films today tell their stories in an extrapolated version of this concept of parallel editing. They show two or three (or more) perspectives of a story throughout intercut in parallel. *The Godfather*, for example, tells its story with four different situations occurring intercut in parallel: (1) Michael Corleone helping his father, (2) rival mob families attacking the Corleone family, (3) Sonny Corleone being angry and getting killed, and (4) Tom Hayden, the Consiglieri, being approached by other mob families and asked to join them. These four different situations intercut in parallel go a long way toward relieving the monotony of just one situation occurring for two hours. It is as if four different stories are better than one.

JUMP CUT

A Jump Cut violates continuity editing. A Jump Cut "jumps" to a different time or place in a scene in a movie and disorients an audience watching it. It can seem like an obvious mistake in editing because it is so unnatural and jarring. Nevertheless, Jean-Luc Godard championed the Jump Cut as a creative device in filmmaking during the 1960s in the French New Wave film *Breathless*. It has become, as a result, a popular editing device for filmmakers ever since. It is used in television commercials and music videos in creative ways especially. In *Breathless*, Jean-Luc Godard used several Jump Cuts during a long scene of a conversation between two actors in a car driving through the streets of Paris. He added the Jump Cuts to add electricity to the scene because the scene by itself was monotonous, too long, and boring.

MONTAGE

Montage is a French word meaning "glue" or "editing." In America, however, *montage* takes on a completely different meaning. *Montage* in America means a scene in a movie that is unlike the rest of the other scenes in a movie, especially the dialog scenes. It occurs when an actor is seen walking across town, for example, from point A to point B, in several different shots, usually without dialog and usually with music playing in the background (as in a "music montage"). The shots of Rocky Balboa running down several different streets in the movie *Rocky*, for example, while preparing for his fight with the heavyweight champion of the world, to Bill Conti's music, is a perfect example of an American montage. An American montage can also condense time in a movie. It can show a lot of different activity from different locations, from the past or present, in a small amount of time on the screen.

KULESHOV EFFECT

The Kuleshov Effect comes from the famous experiment in video editing by Lev Kuleshov in Russia in c.1920. It demonstrated that the juxtaposition of two shots together in a movie, as opposed to one shot by itself, produces the final meaning of a film. This juxtaposition has also been called the essence of cinema. Lev Kuleshov's experiment can be formulated as *shot + shot = emotion*. Lev Kuleshov created a short film with the same shot of a man's face next to a shot of a bowl of soup, a girl in a coffin, and an attractive woman on a couch. An audience watching the film reported that they thought the man was hungry (when seen next to the shot of the soup), sad (when seen next to the shot of the girl in the coffin), and amorous (when seen next to the shot of the attractive woman on the couch). The audience, in other words, connected the two shots juxtaposed together as the ultimate meaning of the film. Editing, and not cinematography, in this way, is what produces the ultimate meaning of a film. Lev Kuleshov's experiment is available for everyone to see for themselves, for free, on Youtube.

MISE EN SCENE

The French term *mise en scene* refers to everything that exists inside a camera frame in a movie, including the set design, the props, the lighting, the actor's blocking (i.e., the actor's positioning) and the actor's movements, etc. It is an omnibus term for *everything* that exists inside a movie screen's frame. However, Andre Bazin, the editor of the influential magazine *Cahiers du Cinema* (*Notebooks on Cinema*) in France during the French New Wave, used the term *mise en scene* to mean something completely different. *Mise en scene*, for Andre Bazin, referred to a scene in a movie that was shot with just one long take, without any editing. It was considered a superior kind of filmmaking because it kept an audience more immersed in a scene than a scene that was edited with multiple wide shots, medium close-ups, and close-ups. Editing, for Andre Bazin, detracts from an audience's ability to stay immersed in a scene, whereas a scene without any editing, with one long take (as in *mise en scene*), improves an audience's ability to stay immersed. It is important to understand that while Soviet montage editing theories before Andre Bazin emphasized the way that editing produces the ultimate meaning of cinema (as in Lev Kuleshov's experiment), Andre Bazin argued in favor of no editing at all. Andre Bazin preferred one long take instead of a scene in a movie edited with wides shots, medium close-ups, and close-ups. *Citizen Kane*, by Orson Welles (and filmed in deep focus by Gregg Toland, the cinematographer), contained a lot of scenes in which the characters in the background, the mid-ground, and the foreground all interacted dramatically together with no editing at all. Andre Bazin preferred this kind of filmmaking (*mise en scene*, with no editing) over editing.

———

EDITING TECHNIQUES

——

CUT ON A BLINK

A natural place to cut on a close-up of an actor's face in a scene in a movie is when an actor blinks, according to Walter Murch in his book *In The Blink of an Eye*. Human beings naturally blink when they have finally understood something, or when they have finally realized something, and this blinking, according to Walter Murch, is a perfect place to cut on a close-up of an actor's face in a scene. It occurs naturally. It is when an actor has finally understood something or realized something, and, of course, there is no more reason for the camera to show the actor's face any longer.

ENTRANCES AND EXITS

Cutting on an actor's entrance in – or exit from – a scene in a movie has been a common practice in Hollywood filmmaking since the very beginning of cinema. A lot of scenes in Hollywood movies start when an actor *enters* a camera's frame and they end when an actor *exists* a camera's frame. Entrances and exits can work equally well in close-up, in fact, when an actor (or an object) enters a camera's frame or exists a camera's frame up close. A close-up of an actor's hand, for example, a foot, or a car bumper entering or exiting a camera's frame in a movie can convey the same idea of a scene beginning or ending as in a full shot of an actor's entire body.

PUNCH-IN

A punch-in is an artificial zoom-in on a person's face in an interview, for example. It usually occurs when a person starts to say something important. It draws the attention of an audience in to the important information and it becomes much more compelling to watch. You can create a punch-in in DaVinci Resolve's *Edit Workspace* by copying a video clip of a person talking in a timeline, putting the copy of the video clip on a layer above the original video clip, increasing the scale (or zoom) of the copy to 120% or so, and trimming the copy of the clip to the point where the person starts to say something important.

B-ROLL

B-Roll is footage that is put on a layer above the normal layer (layer A) of video clips in a timeline. B-Roll footage typically shows what the people in the video clips on layer A are talking about. B-Roll footage, in addition, can hide (or mask) editing mistakes that were made on layer A because the video clips on layer A do not show through the video clips on layer B above. Only the uppermost video clips in a timeline are seen in a final exported film.

RADIO SCRIPT

A Radio Script is an approach to video editing that edits the verbal dialog of a scene first – with an editor's *ears* – and then edits the visual information of the video clips second – with an editor's *eyes*. Dialog in cinema, of course, must always be clear and easy to follow, which means that all of the other audio in a movie, including the SFX and the music, must play quieter than the dialog. The dialog is the most important ingredient in a film's audio – every time, no matter what. Unclear video footage can be tolerated by an audience, but unclear dialog can *never* be tolerated by an audience.

SPLIT EDITS

Split Edits (also known as J and L Cuts) split the audio track from a video clip in a timeline and move the audio (or video) portion of the video clip left or right to be seen or heard above or under a neighboring video clip. Most of the edits in a dialog scene in a movie should use Split Edits because Split Edits increase the ability of an editor to produce natural sounding dialog. Split Edits, in other words, can show the way a character listens to another character's words, without him- or herself ever saying anything in response. Split Edits can also be used creatively when extended and made obvious in a film. In *The Graduate*, for example, by Mike Nichols, Split Edits were used creatively, especially in the transitions to other scenes, which conveyed a sense of advanced craftsmanship in filmmaking for an audience to delight in. You can create Split Edits in DaVinci Resolve's *Edit Workspace* this way.
- Option drag the end of a video clip's audio portion or video portion in a Timeline.
    - This makes the ends of the audio or video portion of a video clip uneven.
- Or detach the audio track of a video clip in a Timeline and drag either the audio portion or the video portion of the clip left or right.

A. Click the Chain Link icon in the Timeline toolbar to unlink (i.e., detach) the audio track from the video clip.
B. Drag the end of either the audio portion or the video portion of the video clip left or right so that it can lay differently underneath (or above) a neighboring video clip.

———

CAMERA SHOTS EDITORS NEED

———

Editors of movies require certain camera shots to be provided by a cinematographer in order to be able to edit a scene successfully. If certain camera shots of a scene are not provided, the editor will not be able to get a scene to flow naturally or work smoothly or normally. One of the cinematographer's jobs, as a result, is to get *exactly* the kinds of shots that will be able to be cut together well in a timeline. The cinematographer would do well to even think ahead of time about what kinds of shots the editor will need. Cinematography and editing are inextricable processes in filmmaking, in this way, because one cannot succeed without the other.

MASTER SCENE TECHNIQUE

The Master Scene Technique in filmmaking is a way of shooting a scene in a movie from many different camera angles and then letting the editor juxtapose the best shots together in a scene in a timeline. The editor will be able to connect a wide variety of different shots together this way, and even experiment with different shot variations, in order to get a scene to work most effectively. An establishing shot (or wide shot) of a scene is usually recorded first by a cinematographer. A set of medium close-ups or over-the-shoulder shots are usually recorded second. A set of close-ups are usually recorded third. And several insert shots or cutaway shots are recorded last.

COVERAGE

Coverage refers to a cinematographer recording as much camera footage (i.e., "coverage") of a scene in a movie as possible, from different camera angles, so that an editor will be able to experiment with different shot juxtapositions in a scene while editing them.

REACTION SHOT

A reaction shot in a movie is a shot that records a character "reacting" to another character's statement or action. Audiences love to see how characters "react" to situations in a movie because their reaction reveals emotional depth and personality. Some film theorists have even argued that *reaction* is more important than *action* in a film. Reacting is the most dramatically interesting thing of all to watch in a movie.

REVERSE ANGLE SHOT

A Reverse Angle Shot is a shot of a situation in a movie from another person's perspective. A chase scene, for example, will typically show a person being chased (looking back at the person giving the chase) in a reverse angle shot. It will show both perspectives of the chase in this way in parallel.

SCREEN DIRECTION

Screen Direction should always be consistent in the shots of a scene in a movie. The actors running in a chase scene, for example, should always run from left to right in order to maintain the continuity of the action of the scene. If one shot showed an actor running from right to left, in the opposite direction, it would contradict the visual message of the scene and not make sense for an audience watching it.

SEGWAY / BRIDGE SHOT

A Segway Shot (a.k.a. Bridge Shot) is a shot in a movie that is placed in between two other shots (or scenes) in a movie which cannot be cut together well in a timeline. It acts as a punctuation mark in the grammar of film language, you could say, breaking up the continuity of the action and therefore allowing completely different shots to follow naturally. A close-up of something, an insert shot of almost anything, even a shot of the clouds in the sky could create a great Segway shot (or a Bridge shot) in order to fit well between two other shots (or scenes) in a movie which cannot be cut together well.

NATURAL WIPE

A Natural Wipe is a Segway or a Bridge Shot in a movie that was recorded during the actual filming of a scene. (An *artificial* wipe transition, by contrast, available in most NLEs today, is not as convincing for audiences to watch as a Natural Wipe.) A Natural Wipe may be created by shooting a close-up of a bus going by in front of a camera while filming a scene, for example, or a person walking directly in front of a camera in a scene, allowing for the subsequent shots to appear on the screen naturally.

180 DEGREE RULE

The 180 Degree Rule in cinematography stipulates that a camera filming a scene in a movie should always stay on one side of an imaginary line dividing the actors of a scene – and *stay* on that same side – so that the same perspective of the scene will be maintained throughout. A shot taken from the other side of the imaginary line would disorient an audience watching it because the shot would have a different background, it would reverse the positions of the actor's faces, and it would degrade the overall immersiveness of the scene.

THE FIVE C'S OF CINEMATOGRAPHY

The Five C's of Cinematography by Joseph Mascelli has been called one of the greatest books on filmmaking ever written. It is a book that is highly recommended for serious filmmakers and for beginning filmmakers alike because it explains the different kinds of shots that fit well in great movies. Joseph Mascelli spent many years in Hollywood cataloging the different kinds of shots that were used in the greatest of Hollywood films, and he described those shots in terms of their visual communication or message. He described how certain shots convey certain meanings in visual storytelling terms and how they have different dramatic purposes. If you want to be a good filmmaker, or a good cinematographer, or even a good film editor, you would do well to learn the different kinds of shots that fit well in the greatest of Hollywood movies, which Joseph Mascelli described so well in *The 5 C's of Cinematography*.

———

TRANSITIONS

———

Film purists argue that transitions should be used only sparingly in a movie because they take an audience out of a film's immersiveness and they draw attention to themselves. They should be used only as visual cues to indicate a change in time or place. In fact, most Hollywood movies do not use transitions at all. They use shots that cut together well instead. There is a popular expression among film editors: "If you can't solve it, dissolve it." But even a dissolve in a movie can seem artificial. Television commercials, marketing promotions, and creative short videos, on the other hand, can use video transitions appropriately and successfully. They can use transitions extremely creatively. DaVinci Resolve contains a large collection of transitions, and third-party transitions can be added to DaVinci Resolve as well.

PREVIEW A TRANSITION
You can preview a Transition between video clips before applying it in a Timeline this way.
1. Effects > Toolbox > Video Transitions > . . . (Options) drop down menu > Hover Scrub Preview
2. Position the playhead between two video clips in a Timeline.
3. Hover the mouse cursor over a Transition listed in Effects > Toolbox > Video Transitions and gently move the mouse cursor from left to right.
    • The Transition will preview in the Source Viewer.

ADD A TRANSITION
You can add a Transition between two video clips in a Timeline this way.
1. Effects > Toolbox > Video Transitions > Drag a transition (such as Cross Dissolve) on top of the ends of two video clips in a Timeline (Figure 49).

2.   Inspector > Transition > Adjust the parameters of the Transition, including its Type, Duration, and/or Ease (Interpolation) > In, Out, In and Out, or Custom, if needed.

- You can resize a Transition manually by zooming into a Transition in a Timeline and dragging its ends.
  - Pro Tip: Some Transitions, such as Cross Dissolve, have different Styles to choose from as well, and their different Styles can only be selected in the Inspector.

Figure 49: Add a Transition   Figure 50: Handle is Missing

DEFAULT TRANSITION

You can use the default Transition in DaVinci Resolve this way.

1.   Select the ends of two neighboring video clips in a Timeline.
2.   Press Command T.

- Pressing Command T places the default Transition of DaVinci Resolve (the Cross Dissolve) between two selected video clips in a Timeline.
- The small red tick on the edge of a Transition listed in Effects > Toolbox > Video Transitions indicates DaVinci Resolve's default transition.

CHANGE DEFAULT TRANSITION

You can change the default Transition in DaVinci Resolve this way.

- Right-click a Transition listed in Effects > Toolbox > Video Transitions > Set as Standard Transition

CORRECT A BROKEN TRANSITION

If a transition applied between two video clips in a Timeline does not work, it is usually because the transition was applied to video clips that lack "handles" (Figure 50). A "handle" is extra footage underneath the ends of a video clip in a Timeline that will allow it to play longer. You can correct a Transition that does not work in DaVinci Resolve this way.

- Manually drag the ends of each video clip inward to hide more of the portion seen in the Timeline and create more space underneath it for handles.

CORRECT A ONE–SIDED TRANSITION

If a transition works only on one video clip in a Timeline, and it is not accepted on a neighboring video clip, the neighboring video clip probably does not have a handle. You can correct a Transition appearing on only one video clip in DaVinci Resolve this way.

- Manually drag the end of the neighboring video clip inward to hide more of the portion seen in the Timeline and create more space underneath it for a handle.

COPY A TRANSITION

You can quickly copy a Transition between two video clips in a Timeline and drop it between two other video clips in the Timeline this way.

- Option-drag the Transition between two video clips and drop it on top of the ends of two other neighboring video clips. (Option-dragging creates a copy of an item automatically.)

FAVORITE A TRANSITION

You can save your favorite Transitions in DaVinci Resolve this way.

1. Effects > Toolbox > Video Transitions > Hover your mouse cursor over a Transition listed.
2. Click the star that appears on the Transition (Figure 51).
   - The Transition will then have a white star placed by its name and appear as a favorite listed in the Favorites section at the bottom of the Effects > Toolbox > Video Transitions list.

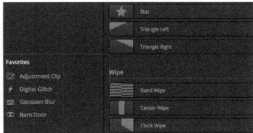

Figure 51: Favorite a Transition   Figure 52: User (Custom) Transitions

CUSTOMIZE A TRANSITION

You can customize a Transition and save it for later reuse in DaVinci Resolve this way.

1. Effects > Toolbox > Video Transitions > Drag a transition on top of the ends of two video clips in a Timeline.
2. Inspector > Transition > Adjust any of the parameters of the Transition, and add keyframes, if needed.
3. Right-click the Transition between the two video clips in the Timeline > Create Transition Preset
4. Name it.
   - Your customized Transition will then appear listed in the User section in the Effects > Toolbox > Video Transitions list (Figure 52).

————

TITLES

———

Titles in DaVinci Resolve include opening titles, end credits, lower thirds, and text that can be used for just about any purpose. Titles in DaVinci Resolve contain some elements that should be understood first, however, before using.

- *Rich Text* is text that can have different text styles applied in the same sentence or in the same text box.
- *Text* + Titles are Titles with parameters that can be keyframed, such as tracking and line spacing, and *Text* + Titles can allow users to create kinetic typography or motion graphics.
- *Effects* can be applied to all text Titles in DaVinci Resolve as well as to video clips. The vast collection of Effects in DaVinci Resolve can make text in Titles look extremely creative and professional. Effects can be keyframed on and off as well to provide an editor with complete control of when they occur and how intensely they appear.
- *Text Mask* is a way of getting imagery (video clips or graphics files) to appear inside letters.

PREVIEW A TITLE
You can preview a Title (before applying it) in DaVinci Resolve this way.

1. Effects > Toolbox > Titles > . . . (Options) drop down menu > Hover Scrub Preview
2. Hover your mouse cursor and slowly drag it over a Title listed in the Effects > Toolbox > Titles Panel.
   - Its Text and animation will display in the Source Viewer.

ADD A TITLE
You can add a Title to a Timeline in DaVinci Resolve this way.

1. Effects > Toolbox > Titles > Drag a Title to a Timeline (Figure 53).

Figure 53: Add a Title   Figure 54: Apply an Effect to a Title

- You can drag a Title over a blank area of a Timeline to use it with a black background or you can drag a Title over a video clip in a Timeline to use the video clip as a background.

2. Inspector > Video > Title > Text > Type your own text into the text box provided.
3. Inspector > Video > Title > Text > Adjust the Size, Font, Color, Tracking, Line Spacing, and other options of your Title's text.
   - Pro Tip: A Text + Title can have keyframes added to its parameters in the Inspector in order to create kinetic typography or motion graphics.

ADD AN EFFECT TO A TITLE

You can apply an Effect to a Text + Title in DaVinci Resolve this way. (Effects work on Text + Titles, not plain Text Titles.)

1. Effects > Toolbox > Titles > Text + > Drag a Text + Title to a Timeline.
2. Inspector > Video > Title > Text + > Type your own text in the text box provided.
3. Inspector > Video > Title > Text + > Adjust the Size, Font, Color, Tracking, Line Spacing, and other options of your Text + Title's text.
4. Effects > Open FX > Drag an Effect on top of the Text + Title in the Timeline (Figure 54).
5. Inspector > Effects > Effect Name > Adjust the parameters of the Effect.
   - Pro Tip: Effects that work especially well with the Text + Titles in DaVinci Resolve are Digital Glitch, Directional Blur, Mosaic, and Flicker; however, there are many, many other Effects that work very well.
   - Pro Tip: Most Effects on Text + Titles can be keyframed on and off in the Inspector to provide an editor with complete control over when they occur and how intensely they appear.

TEXT MASK SIMULATION

A text mask allows imagery (a video clip or a graphics file) to appear inside letters. An easy way to "simulate" a text mask in DaVinci Resolve is to apply a Blend Mode to a video clip on a track above a Title in a Timeline. The Multiply Blend Mode will "blend" the pixels of the video clip with the pixels of the Title on the track below. You can simulate a text mask with a Blend Mode in DaVinci Resolve this way.

1. Effects > Toolbox > Titles > Drag a Title onto a track in a Timeline.
2. Place a video clip (preferably a visually interesting video clip such as fire or a timelapse shot of clouds) on a track above (not below) the Title in the Timeline.
3. Select the Title in the Timeline.
4. Inspector > Video > Title > Text > Type your own text in the text box provided.
5. Inspector > Video > Title > Text > Adjust the Size, Font, Color (white text is required for a text mask simulation, and an extra bold text style works especially well), Tracking, Line Spacing, and other options of your Title's text.
6. Select the video clip on the track above the Title in the Timeline.
7. Inspector > Video > Composite > Composite Mode > Select a Composite Mode (i.e., a Blend Mode) such as Multiply (Figure 55).
   - "Composites" are "Blend Modes" in DaVinci Resolve.
     - Pro Tip: The Multiply Blend Mode simulates a text mask very well, but you can cycle through all of the other Blend Modes in the Inspector and observe their individual effects in the Timeline Viewer as well this way.
       - Select one Blend Mode first and then press the up or down Arrow keys to cycle through all of the other Blend Modes.

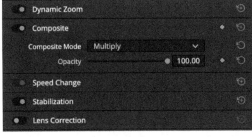
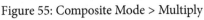

Figure 55: Composite Mode > Multiply   Figure 56: Fade a Title In and Out

FADE A TITLE IN / OUT

You can fade a Title in or out in a Timeline in DaVinci Resolve this way.

1. Hover the mouse cursor over the top edge of a Title added to a Timeline.
2. Drag the small white boxes that appear in the top right or left corners of the Title inward (Figure 56).
    - A Tool Tip shows the number of frames dragged inward to let you create a short fade or a long fade.

CUSTOMIZE A TITLE

You can create a customized Title and save it for later reuse in DaVinci Resolve this way.

1. Effects > Toolbox > Titles > Drag a Title to a Timeline.
2. Inspector > Video > Title > Text > Type your own text in the text box provided.
3. Inspector > Video > Title > Text > Adjust the Size, Font, Color, Tracking, Line Spacing, and other options of your Title's text.
4. Drag the Title from the Timeline into a Power Bin that you have set up in the Media Pool (Figure 57).
    - Power Bins are folders that contain reusable items for all projects in DaVinci Resolve. (Please see *Power Bins* in the *Media Pool* chapter of *DaVinci Resolve Editing Step By Step Instructions* for an explanation of how to set up a Power Bin.)

Figure 57: Save a Custom Title

Figure 58: Title with a Transparent Background

TRANSPARENT BACKGROUND

You can create a Title with a transparent background – for use in other videos – in DaVinci Resolve this way.

1. Effects > Toolbox > Titles > Drag a Title to a Timeline.
2. Inspector > Video > Title > Text > Type your own text in the text box provided.
3. Inspector > Video > Title > Text > Adjust the Size, Font, Color, Tracking, Line Spacing, and other options of your Title's text.
4. Place *in* and *out* points around the Title you created in the Timeline for export.

- Position the playhead at the start of the Title and press I on the keyboard to set an *in* point. Position the playhead at the end of the Title and press O on the keyboard to set an *out* point.

5. Deliver workspace > Custom Export > Export Video >
    A. Format > Quicktime
    B. Codec > Apple ProRes
    C. Type > Apple ProRes 4444 (Figure 58)
    D. Click the Export Alpha checkbox on.
    E. Add to Render Que
    F. Render
        - Apple's ProRes 4444 format supports Alpha Channels for transparent backgrounds.

———

VIDEO TRANSFORMATIONS

———

DaVinci Resolve has a wide range of video transformation effects that can be applied to video clips in a Timeline: Auto Color, Sharpening, Widescreen, Speed Changes (Retiming), Speed Ramping, Dynamic Zoom, Masking, and a host of Transform controls. Video transformation effects are procedures that require altering a video clip in several steps in DaVinci Resolve. By contrast, Effects in DaVinci Resolve – such as Gaussian Blur, Watercolor, or Digital Glitch – are self-contained effects that can be dropped onto a video clip in a Timeline in one step. (Effects in DaVinci Resolve are explained in the *Effects* chapter of *DaVinci Resolve Editing Step By Step Instructions*.)

AUTO COLOR
You can quickly correct the colors of a video clip according to DaVinci Resolve's professional color standard this way.

1. Select a video clip in a Timeline in the Edit workspace of DaVinci Resolve.
2. Switch to the Color workspace.
   - Click the Color workspace icon at the bottom of the DaVinci Resolve user interface.
      A. In the Color workspace, above the Color Wheels, click the letter A with a circle around it (this is Auto Color Balance – Figure 59).
         - The video clip's colors will automatically be corrected according to DaVinci Resolve's professional color standard.
   - Pro Tip: You can further correct a video clip's exposure (i.e., tone) in the Color workspace. (But this, of course, is not always necessary.)
      - Drag the Exposure Slider next to the Offset Color Wheel up or down.

- You can also drag the Exposure Sliders next to each of the Lift, Gamma, and Gain Color Wheels up or down to adjust each of their individual exposure ranges. (This may take a lot of time, however, and it, of course, is not always necessary.)
  - Pro Tip: You can see "before" and "after" versions of your settings by clicking the Bypass icon at the top of the Viewer on and off.

Figure 59: Auto Color

Figure 60: Sharpen

SHARPEN

You can sharpen a video clip in DaVinci Resolve this way.

1. Select a video clip in a Timeline in the Edit workspace of DaVinci Resolve.
2. Switch to the Color workspace.
   - Click the Color workspace icon at the bottom of the DaVinci Resolve user interface.
     - A. In the Color workspace, right-click the node that automatically appears in the node graph > Add Node > Add Serial.
     - B. Select the Serial Node you have just created in the node graph.
     - C. Click the Blur icon above the Curves Panel at the bottom middle of the Color workspace's user interface, then click the Sharpen icon in the Blur panel.
       - I. In the Blur/Sharpen area, drag the Radius slider down (Figure 60).
       - II. Increase the Level percentage.
       - III. Increase the Coring Softness percentage.
         - Be careful not to over-sharpen a video.
           - Pro Tip: You can see "before" and "after" versions of your settings by clicking the Bypass icon at the top of the Viewer on and off.

Figure 61: Stabilization

Figure 62: Widescreen (Output Blanking 2.40)

STABILIZE

DaVinci Resolve's Stabilize feature is one of the best stabilizing features in the video editing industry. It has a Camera Lock component that can make a shaky video look as if it was shot on a locked down tripod without any shaking at all. You can add extra tracking points to a shaky video clip as well in the Stabilize feature in DaVinci Resolve's Color workspace to make a shaky video look absolutely perfect. You can use the Stabilize feature in DaVinci Resolve this way.

1. Select a video clip in a Timeline that you want to stabilize.
    - Pro Tip: It is well-advised to resize (i.e., trim) a shaky video clip with the Razor Blade Tool to the smallest length it can possibly be before stabilizing it. Why? Stabilizing a video clip's entire length, with its wildly varying degrees of shakiness, can throw off the Analyze function of the Stabilize feature in DaVinci Resolve and possibly render stabilization useless.
2. Inspector > Video > Stabilization (Figure 61)
    A. Mode >
        - Perspective = analyzes pan, tilt, zoom, and rotate movements.
        - Similarity = analyzes pan, tilt, and rotate movements.
        - Translation = analyzes pan and tilt movements only.
    B. Camara Lock = creates a 100% stable video clip that does not have any movement in it at all. However, it can zoom the edges of a video clip in quite a bit in order to hide the black edges it creates. (Using Camera Lock is not always required for all video clips, of course.)
    C. Zoom = enlarges a video clip's output to hide the black edges created by the Camera Lock function.
    D. Cropping Ratio Slider = sets the percentage of cropping used to compensate for stabilization.
    E. Smooth = smoothes out the stabilization process overall.
    F. Strength = sets the overall strength of the stabilization process.

G. Click the Stabilize button when all of your Stabilize settings have been set.
- Please Note: Each newly adjusted stabilization setting requires the Stabilize button to be clicked again before any new stabilization setting can take effect.
  - Pro Tip: You can also stabilize a shaky video clip in several iterations (or generations), if needed.
    I. First, stabilize a shaky video clip.
    II. Select the stabilized video clip in the Timeline.
    III. Export it.
    IV. Import this stabilized video clip.
    V. Stabilize it again.
    VI. Repeat this process over and over, if needed.

WIDESCREEN

The Widescreen control in DaVinci Resolve can be applied to a Timeline this way.
1. Timeline Menu > Output Blanking > 2.40 (Figure 62)
2. Adjust the vertical position of each video clip in the Timeline in the Inspector so that each video clip will fit well underneath the black bars that Output Blanking creates at the top and bottom of the Timeline.
   A. Select a video clip in the Timeline.
   B. Inspector > Video > Transform > Position > Drag the Y field up or down to reposition the video clip well underneath the black bars created by the Output Blanking.

TRANSFORM CONTROLS

The Timeline Viewer's Transform controls allow videos, titles, and graphics files to be transformed manually in the Timeline Viewer. Videos, titles, and graphics files can be moved, resized, cropped, rotated, and have their pitch and yaw adjusted in faux 3D space, if needed, to give an editor complete control over their final appearance. You can use the Transform controls in the Timeline Viewer in DaVinci Resolve this way.
1. Select a video clip, title, or graphics file in a Timeline.
2. Select Transform from the drop down menu at the bottom of the Timeline Viewer.
   - A bounding box will appear around the video clip, title, or graphics file selected in the Timeline (Figure 63).
   - The corners and edges of the bounding box can be dragged manually to resize the video clip, title, or graphics file inside.

- The parameters of the bounding box can also be adjusted in the Inspector (with precise mathematical control).
    - Pro Tip: You can improve your view of a bounding box in the Timeline Viewer by decreasing the Timeline Viewer's view from Fit to a percentage size smaller. You can also make the Timeline Viewer bigger in the DaVinci Resolve user interface by dragging its edges out and dragging the edges of its neighboring panels in.
    - Pro Tip: You can drag an item inside a bounding box in the Timeline Viewer's screen in a straight line by Shift-dragging it.
    - Pro Tip: You can toggle the bounding box in the Timeline Viewer on or off to see more clearly how your adjustments finally look this way.
        - View > Viewer Overlay > Toggle On/Off (Shift Tilde).

Figure 63: Transform Controls   Figure 64: Dynamic Zoom

DYNAMIC ZOOM

The Dynamic Zoom function in DaVinci Resolve is similar to the Ken Burns effect in Final Cut Pro editing software. It zooms a video clip in or out, or to a another position within the frame, and it allows a video clip to be recomposed easily. It creates a moving camera effect artificially, and yet it looks professional and smooth and steady. You can also create a pan-and-scan effect using the Dynamic Zoom function. Animating still photographs in or out, or across the screen, with the Dynamic Zoom function is especially useful because it alleviates the stationary look of still photographs and makes them dynamic. The Dynamic Zoom function in DaVinci Resolve can also make a video look as if it was shot using professional camera equipment such as dollies, gimbals, or cranes. You can use the Dynamic Zoom function in DaVinci Resolve this way.

1. Select a video clip, title, or graphics file in a Timeline.
    - It will appear in the Timeline Viewer.

2. Select Dynamic Zoom from the drop down menu at the bottom of the Timeline Viewer.
3. Two rectangles will appear on the Timeline Viewer's screen:
    - Green Rectangle = start of zoom.
    - Red Rectangle = end of zoom.
4. Move and resize the green rectangle on the Timeline Viewer's screen to where you want the Dynamic Zoom to start (Figure 64).
5. Move and resize the red rectangle on the Timeline Viewer's screen to where you want the Dynamic Zoom to end.
    - Pro Tip: You can set the interpolation (movement style) of the Dynamic Zoom, if you want, in the Inspector as well.
        - Inspector > Dynamic Zoom Ease > (Figure 65)
            - Linear = straight non-stop movement.
            - Ease In = slow to start movement.
            - Ease Out = slow to end movement.
            - Ease In and Out = both slow to start and slow to end movement.
                - Pro Tip: While the Dynamic Zoom Effect must be applied to the entire length of a video clip in a Timeline, you can alternatively use keyframes to manually adjust the Scale (Zoom) and/or the Position of a video clip (Y or Z) in the Inspector instead if you want to get a video clip to zoom or pan at any speed, in any direction, or for any duration. (Keyframes are explained in the *Keyframes* chapter of *DaVinci Resolve Editing Step By Step Instructions*.)

BLEND MODES

A video clip can have its pixels "blended" with the pixels of a video clip on a track below in a Timeline in DaVinci Resolve. This can create an amazing visual effect with amazing color combinations. You can add a Blend Mode to a video clip in a Timeline in DaVinci Resolve this way.

1. Add a video clip on a track above the other video clips in a Timeline.
2. Select the video clip on the track above.
3. Inspector > Video > Composite > Select a Blend Mode from the Composite Mode drop down list (Figure 66).
    - "Composites" are "Blend Modes" in DaVinci Resolve.
4. Adjust the Opacity of the video clip on the track above to change the amount of the Composite's (i.e., Blend Mode's) effect.

- The Opacity Slider is located under the Composite drop down menu in the Inspector.
  - Pro Tip: You can cycle through all of the Blend Modes available in the Inspector in DaVinci Resolve and preview how they each look in the Timeline Viewer this way.
    - A. First, click a Blend Mode from the Composite drop down list in the Inspector.
    - B. Second, press the down arrow key on the keyboard to cycle through all of the other Blend Modes available.
    - C. You can view how each Blend Mode looks in the Timeline Viewer as you cycle through all of the different Blend Modes.
      - Some Blend Modes, you will find, look better than others.

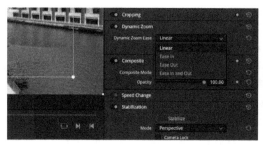

Figure 65: Dynamic Zoom > Ease In/Out

Figure 66: Composite Modes (Blend Modes)

CHANGE A VIDEO CLIP'S SPEED

You can change a video clip's speed (to slow motion or to fast motion [timelapse]) in DaVinci Resolve this way.

- Right-click a video clip in a Timeline > Change Clip Speed (Figure 67) > Speed Field > Add the percentage of the change in speed you want.
  - Normal speed = 100%
  - Slow motion = 30% or so.
  - Fast motion (timelapse) = 200% or so.
    - Experiment with different percentages of speed changes to see what speed works best.
      - Pro Tip: You can render the video clip when done for smoother playback.
        - Right-click the video clip > Render in Place (Figure 68)

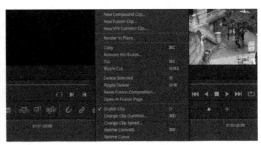

Figure 67: Change Clip Speed   Figure 68: Render in Place

CHANGE A VIDEO CLIP'S SPEED (INSPECTOR)
You can change a video clip's speed (to slow motion or to fast motion [timelapse]) in the Inspector in DaVinci Resolve this way.
1. Select a video clip in a Timeline.
2. Inspector > Video > Speed Change > Add the percentage of the change in speed you want (Figure 69).
   - Normal speed = 100%
   - Slow motion = 30% or so.
   - Fast motion (timelapse) = 400% or so.
     - Experiment with different percentages of speed changes to see what speed works best.
       - Pro Tip: You can render the video clip when done for smoother playback.
         - Right-click the video clip > Render in Place

FREEZE FRAME
You can create a Freeze Frame in a video clip in DaVinci Resolve this way.
1. Position the playhead over a video clip in a Timeline where you want to create a Freeze Frame.
2. Right-click the video clip > Change Clip Speed > Click the checkbox next to Freeze Frame.
3. Set the duration of the Freeze Frame.
   A. Splice the Freeze Framed clip with the Razor Blade Tool where you want the Freeze Frame to stop.
   B. Right-click the video clip that was created after the splice made by the Razor Blade Tool > Change Clip Speed > Uncheck the checkbox next to Freeze Frame.

REVERSE A VIDEO CLIP
You can reverse a video clip so that it will play backward in DaVinci Resolve this way.

Figure 69: Inspector > Speed Change

Figure 70: Retime Controls

- Right-click a video clip in a Timeline > Change Clip Speed > Click the check box next to Reverse.
    - or Inspector > Speed Change > Direction > Select the Reverse Double Arrows icon.

RETIME A VIDEO CLIP

You can retime a video clip with the Retime Controls in DaVinci Resolve this way.
1. Right-click a video clip in a Timeline > Retime Controls (Figure 70)
    - A Retime Bar appears on top of the video clip in the Timeline.
2. Change the video clip's speed manually.
    - Drag the Retime Bar's end on top of the video clip.
        - Its percentage of change will appear in the Retime Bar.
        - or Select a percentage of speed change from the drop down menu in the Retime Bar.
            - Pro Tip: You can also Freeze Frame or Reverse a video clip by selecting Freeze Frame or Reverse from the drop down menu in the Retime Bar. Drag the second Freeze Frame bar on the video clip to adjust the Freeze Frame's duration.
    - Triangles on the Retime Bar mean the following:
        - Blue Triangles = 100% speed.
        - Yellow Triangles = changed speed.
        - Closely Placed Triangles = fast speed.
        - Loosely Placed Triangles = slow speed.
        - Red Triangle = freeze frame.

RETIME PROCESSING (RENDERING)

There are different ways that DaVinci Resolve can process (i.e., render) a retimed video clip, and some retiming processes work better than others. You can select different Retime Processes in DaVinci Resolve this way.
1. Select a video clip in a Timeline that has been retimed.

2. Inspector > Video > Retime and Scaling > Retime Process (Figure 71)
   - Nearest = duplicates frames for slow motion.
   - Frame Blend = dissolves duplicate frames (use this when Optical Flow produces strange results).
   - Optical Flow = estimates and duplicates the motion between frames.
     - This works well with linear motion in a video clip. It works badly, however, with several different kinds of motion in a video clip.
     - Motion Estimation (Optical Flow's further settings).
       - Standard (Faster or Better).
       - Enhanced (Faster or Better).
       - Speed Warp (Studio only). Speed Warp is the highest quality setting of Optical Flow, and it makes slow motion look extremely smooth.
     - Pro Tip: When done, you can render the retimed video clip so that it will playback smoothly.
       - Right-click the retimed video clip > Render in Place

Figure 71: Retime Processing

Figure 72: Retime Bar on top of a Video Clip

SPEED RAMP

Changing the speed of a video clip is linear. It is constant. The video clip itself will play back at its changed speed without variation. Ramping the speed of a video clip, on the other hand, is variable. Speed Ramping creates multiple speed changes in a video clip with animation curves to smooth out their divisions. You can create Speed Ramps in a video clip in DaVinci Resolve this way.

1. Position the playhead over a video clip in a Timeline where you want to create a speed point.
2. Right click the video clip > Retime Controls
   - A Retime Bar appears on top of the video clip (Figure 72).
3. Click the drop down menu in the Retime Bar > Add Speed Point

- This sets a speed point located where the playhead is parked (Figure 73).
4. Add a second speed point.
    A. Reposition the playhead where you want to create a second speed point in the video clip.
    B. Click the drop down menu in the Retime Bar > Add Speed Point
        - You can create as many speed points as you like by repeating the steps described above.
5. Alter the speed that exists between two speed points.
    - Drag their speed points.
6. Delete a Speed Point, if needed.
    A. Select a speed point.
    B. Click the drop down menu in the Retime Bar > Clear Speed Point

Figure 73: Speed Points on a Video Clip

Figure 74: Speed Ramp Curves

SPEED RAMP CURVES

After creating a speed ramped video clip, you can adjust the animation curves (and the keyframes involved) to smoothly alternate between the different speed divisions used. This provides better control of the different speed ramp sections and their interaction. You can adjust the animation curves (and keyframes) of the speed points of a video clip with a Speed Ramp applied in DaVinci Resolve this way.

1. Select a video clip in a Timeline with a Speed Ramp applied to it.
2. Show the Curves Editor underneath the video clip with a Speed Ramp (Figure 74).
    - Right click the video clip > Retime Curve
3. Change a curve point.
    A. Select a curve point in the Curve Editor.
    B. Click the Bezier or Linear curve point icons at the top of the Curve Editor to change a curve point.

- Linear curve points have only straight lines between them. They create one constant speed without variation, and they look abrupt.
  - Pro Tip: You can drag the curve points that exist in the Curve Editor to rearrange the position and value of each one directly.
- Bezier curve points have curved lines between them. They create smoothly changing speeds without abrupt starts or stops.
  - Pro Tip: You can enlarge or minimize a Bezier point's animation curve for greater control. First select the curve point and then drag the red handle that appears underneath it.

———

EFFECTS

———

There are 3 kinds of Effects that can be applied to video clips in DaVinci Resolve: Open Effects, Resolve Effects, and Fusion Effects. Third party effects can also be purchased online and added to DaVinci Resolve as plugins. Effects can be applied to an individual video clip directly or to an Adjustment Clip on top of a video clip non-destructively. An Adjustment Clip affects the video clip below it but leaves the video clip itself untouched. Keyframes, as well, can be added to Effects on a video clip to provide full control over when an Effect occurs and how intensely it appears. DaVinci Resolve has useful Generators, in addition – such as Solid Color, Paper, and Texture – which can be used in conjunction with Effects, used with composites, or used as separate backgrounds by themselves.

SEARCH AN EFFECT
You can search for an Effect in DaVinci Resolve this way.
- Effects > Open FX (or Toolbox > Effects) > Click the Magnifying Glass Search icon > Type an Effect's name in the Effects search bar that appears (Figure 75).
  - Please Note: The Effects search bar must be cleared before you can see the entire list of Effects again.
    - Click the X in the search bar to clear the search bar.

PREVIEW AN EFFECT
You can preview an Effect before applying it to a video clip in DaVinci Resolve this way.
1. Effects > Open FX > . . . (Options) drop down menu > Hover Scrub Preview
2. Select a video clip in a Timeline that you want to preview an Effect on.
3. Effects > Open FX > Hover your mouse cursor over an effect listed.

- The Effect will preview in the Source Viewer.

ADD AN EFFECT
You can add an Effect to a video clip in DaVinci Resolve this way.
1. Effects > Open FX > Drag an Effect on top of a video clip in a Timeline.
2. Inspector > Effects > Adjust the Effect's parameters.
   - Pro Tip: You can keyframe the parameters of an Effect on a video clip to better control when the parameters occur and how intensely they appear. (Please see *Add Keyframes to an Effect* below.)

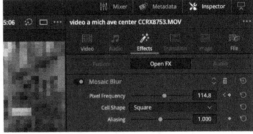

Figure 75: Search for an Effect   Figure 76: Remove an Effect

REMOVE AN EFFECT
You can remove an Effect from a video clip in DaVinci Resolve this way.
1. Select a video clip in a Timeline with an Effect applied to it.
2. Inspector > Effects > Effect Name > Click the trash can icon next to the Effect's name (Figure 76).

ON SCREEN CONTROLS
Some Effects in DaVinci Resolve (such as the 3D Keyer Effect for Green Screen) require the On Screen Controls to be activated in the Timeline Viewer in order to work. You can activate the On Screen Controls of an Effect in DaVinci Resolve this way.
1. Effects > Open FX > Drag an Effect on top of a video clip in a Timeline.
2. Timeline Viewer's drop down menu > Open FX Overlay (Figure 77)

Figure 77: On Screen Controls > Open FX   Figure78: Render in Place

EFFECT PARAMETERS

The parameters of Effects in DaVinci Resolve can be adjusted in the Inspector this way.

- Inspector > Effects tab > Effect Name > Adjust any of the parameters listed with an Effect.
  - Pro Tip: The individual parameters of an Effect in DaVinci Resolve can be keyframed for greater control over when they occur and how intensely they appear. (Please see *Add Keyframes to an Effect* below.)

TOGGLE AN EFFECT ON / OFF

Toggling an Effect on or off is a useful way of seeing how an Effect on a video clip (or a Title) actually looks. It is a way of seeing "before" and "after" versions of the Effect to improve your overall perception of it.

- Inspector > Effects tab > Effect Name > Click the red dot next to an Effect's Name on or off.

REORDER EFFECTS

The order of Effects applied to a video clip (or a Text + title) in a Timeline in DaVinci Resolve can have a big impact on how Effects ultimately look. You can rearrange the order of Effects on a video clip (or a Text + title) in DaVinci Resolve this way.

- Inspector > Effects > Effect Name > Click the Up or Down Arrow on an Effect's title bar to get the Effect to move up or down.

FAVORITE AN EFFECT

You can save your favorite Effects in DaVinci Resolve this way.

- Effects > Open FX > Click the star icon that appears when you hover the mouse cursor over an effect listed.
  - A starred Effect will then appear listed in the Favorite area at the bottom of the Effects list.

CUSTOMIZE AN EFFECT

You can customize and save a customized Effect in DaVinci Resolve this way.

1. Effects > Toolbox > Effects > Drag an Adjustment Clip above a video clip in a Timeline that you want to add an Effect to.
2. Effects > Open FX > Drag an Effect on top of the Adjustment Clip.
3. Inspector > Effects > Effect Name > Adjust the parameters of the Effect on the Adjustment Clip.
4. Add keyframes if needed.

5. When done, drag the Adjustment Clip with the Effect on it into a Power Bin that has been set up in the Media Pool. (Please see *Power Bins* in the *Media Pool* chapter of *DaVinci Resolve Editing Step By Step Instructions* for a full explanation of how to set up a Power Bin.)

RENDER AN EFFECT

You can Render an Effect on a video clip (or a Title) in a Timeline in DaVinci Resolve so that it will play back more smoothly this way.

- Right-click a video clip (or a Text + title) with an Effect applied to it > Render in Place (Figure 78)

EFFECT ON AN ADJUSTMENT CLIP

An Adjustment Clip in DaVinci Resolve is a blank video clip that can hold Effects that will affect all video clips below it in a Timeline. It is a convenient way of applying an Effect to a video clip without having to affect the actual video clip itself. It is non-destructive. It can be deactivated or deleted or copied or moved around in a Timeline at any time. You can add an Effect to an Adjustment Clip in DaVinci Resolve this way.

1. Effects > Toolbox > Effects > Drag an Adjustment Clip to a track above the other video clips in a Timeline that you want to apply an Effect to (Figure 79).
2. Effects > Open FX > Drag an Effect on top of the Adjustment Clip in the Timeline.
3. Inspector > Effects > Effect Name > Adjust the parameters of the Effect that was applied to the Adjustment Clip.
   - Pro Tip: You can toggle an Adjustment Clip on or off to see its "before" and "after" versions by deactivating it and reactivating it repeatedly.
     A. Click the Adjustment Clip to select it.
     B. Press D.
       - This deactivates (or dims) the Adjustment Clip.
     C. To reactivate the Adjustment Clip.
       - Press D again.

Figure 79: Adjustment Clip

Figure 80: Keyframe an Effect

EFFECT ON A TITLE

Effects can be applied to Text + titles in DaVinci Resolve as well as to video clips. In fact, Effects on Text + titles can open up the full potential of text in DaVinci Resolve and make Titles look extremely professional and creative. You can apply an Effect to a Text + title in DaVinci Resolve this way.

1. First add a Title to a Timeline in DaVinci Resolve.
    A. Effects > Toolbox > Titles > Drag the Text + title to a Timeline.
    B. Inspector > Video > Text + > Type your own text in the text box provided.
    C. Inspector > Video > Text + > Adjust the Size, Font, Color, Tracking, and Line Spacing options of your Text + title.
2. Effects > Open FX > Drag an Effect on top of the Text + title in the Timeline.
    - Pro Tip: Effects that work especially well with Text + titles in DaVinci Resolve are Digital Glitch, Directional Blur, Mosaic, and Flicker; however, there are many, many other Effects that work very well with Text + titles.
    - Pro Tip: You can add keyframes to an Effect on a Text + title in a Timeline to control when an Effect occurs and how intensely it appears. (See *Add Keyframes to an Effect* below.)

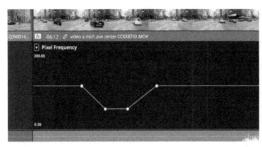

Figure 81: Keyframe Editor

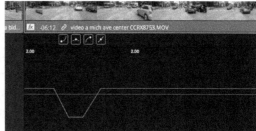

Figure 82: Curve Editor

KEYFRAME AN EFFECT

You can add keyframes to an Effect applied to a video clip (or to a Text + title) in DaVinci Resolve this way.

1. Effects > Open FX > Drag an Effect on top of a video clip (or a Text + title) in a Timeline.
2. Position the playhead on top of the video clip (or a Text + title) with the Effect in the Timeline where you want to add a keyframe.
3. Inspector > Effects > Effect Name > Adjust the value (i.e., amount) of one of the Effect's parameters (Figure 80).

4. Inspector > Effects > Effect Name > Click the diamond icon at the far end of the parameter that had its value adjusted (Figure 80).
   - This will set the first keyframe on the parameter. The diamond icon will turn red. This means the Effect's parameter has a keyframe active on it.
5. Reposition the playhead on top of the video clip in the Timeline where you want to add a second keyframe.
6. Inspector > Effects > Effect Name > Readjust the value (i.e., amount) of the parameter that you previously set a keyframe to.
   - A second keyframe will be added to this value automatically.
     - Please Note: Second keyframes in DaVinci Resolve are added automatically whenever you move the playhead and adjust the parameter you previously set a keyframe to. Why? To make it easier to apply keyframes when you have a lot of keyframes to apply. However, if this is confusing because it is so unintuitive, you can add the second keyframe manually in the same way that you added the first keyframe. (Please see the *Keyframes* chapter in *DaVinci Resolve Editing Step By Step Instructions* for a full explanation of keyframes.)
7. Repeat the above steps to add further keyframes.
   - Pro Tip: You can use the Keyframe/Curve Editor to adjust the keyframes with even greater control (Figure 81, 82).
     - Click the Keyframe/Curve Editor icon (i.e., the the curvy line between the two diamonds icon) at the bottom of a video clip in a Timeline that has a keyframe on it (or Clip > Show Curve Editor). This will open up the Keyframe/Curve Editor underneath the video clip. (Please see the *Keyframes* chapter in *DaVinci Resolve Editing Step By Step Instructions* for a full explanation of the Keyframe/Curve Editor.)
       - Zoom in on the video clip in the Timeline in order to see the Keyframe Selection Drop Down Arrow in the top left corner of the Keyframe/Curve Editor. Then select the keyframes that you created from the keyframes list.
         - The keyframes that you created will become visible as white squares in the Keyframe/Curve editor, and they can be dragged around in any direction.

SHOW VIDEO CLIPS WITH EFFECTS
You can see which video clip in a Timeline has an Effect applied to it in DaVinci Resolve this way.
- An FX Badge appears on the bottom left corner of each video clip with an Effect in a Timeline.

PASTE ATTRIBUTES
To quickly adjust a lot of video clips in a Timeline with the same settings from the Inspector that have been applied to one video clip, you can use the Paste Attributes feature in DaVinci Resolve to do so.
1. Select a video clip in a Timeline that has attributes from the Inspector that you want to copy onto other video clips.
2. Press Command C to copy the video clip's attributes from the Inspector.
3. Right-click the other video clips in the Timeline that you want to apply those same attributes to > Paste Attributes
4. Select the checkboxes in the Paste Attributes dialog box that you want to paste onto the other video clips.
5. Click Apply.

REMOVE ATTRIBUTES
You can remove attributes from the Inspector from a video clip in DaVinci Resolve this way.
1. Right-click a video clip in a Timeline that has attributes from the Inspector that you want to remove > Remove Attributes
2. Deselect (i.e., uncheck) the checkboxes of the attributes from the Inspector in the Paste Attributes dialog box that you want to remove.
3. Click Apply.

THIRD PARTY EFFECTS
You can search online for third-party Effects and add (and Manage) third-party Effects in DaVinci Resolve this way.
- Search online for third-party Effects that DaVinci Resolve can accept as plugins.
  - OpenFX plugins are especially popular with DaVinci Resolve users.
- DaVinci Resolve Menu > Preferences > System > Video Plugins / Audio Plugins > Enable All / Disable All, Add / Remove > Save

GREEN SCREEN
You can use the Green Screen Effect to remove the green background in a video clip in DaVinci Resolve this way.

1. Import a video clip that contains a green background into a Timeline in DaVinci Resolve. (Free green screen video clips can be searched for and downloaded from the internet, and you can create your own video clips with green backgrounds as well.)
2. Effects > Toolbox > Open FX > Drag the 3D Keyer Effect on top of the video clip in the Timeline that has a green background.
3. Timeline Viewer > Select the Open FX Overlay from the drop down menu at the bottom of the Timeline Viewer.
4. In the Timeline Viewer, drag the mouse cursor on a green area of the video clip.
   - Its green area will disappear.
5. Zoom in further and drag a second time on a green area closer to the edge of an object in the video clip.
   - Even more green area (closer to the edge of an object) will disappear.
6. Inspector > Effects > 3D Keyer > Drag the Despill slider to activate Despill.
   - This will remove the green fringing (spillover from the green screen's bright light) off the objects in the video.
     - Pro Tip: You can create an even cleaner green screen effect with the Matte Finesse sliders in the 3D Keyer Effect in the Inspector.
       - A. The Clean Black Slider sharpens the edges of black (i.e., dark) objects.
       - B. The Clean White Slider sharpens the edges of white (i.e., light) objects.
7. Timeline Viewer > Deselect the OpenFX On Screen Control from the Timeline Viewer's drop down menu when you are done. Select the default "Transform" On Screen Control when done (Figure 83).

DIGITAL GLITCH
You can use the Digital Glitch Effect in DaVinci Resolve this way.
1. Effects > Toolbox > Effects > Drag an Adjustment Clip onto a track above another video clip (or a Text + title) in a Timeline.
2. Shorten the Adjustment Clip to about 8 frames or so.
3. Effects > Toolbox > Effects > Fusion Effects > Drag the Digital Glitch Effect on top of the Adjustment Clip in the Timeline (Figure 84).
4. Inspector > Effects > Digital Glitch > Adjust the Digital Glitch Effect's parameters if needed. (The default settings of the Digital Glitch Effect, however, work very well on their own.)
5. Copy the Adjustment Clip several times in the Timeline and put the copies of it over other areas of the video clip (or Text + title).

- Option-drag the Adjustment Clip several times. (Option-dragging creates a copy of an item automatically.)

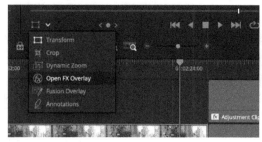

Figure 83: Open FX/Transform

Figure 84: Digital Glitch in Effects

FAUX LENS FLARE

You can create a faux Lens Flare Effect on a video clip (or a Text + title) in DaVinci Resolve this way.

1. Effects > Open FX > Resolve FX Light > Drag the Glow Effect on top of a video clip (or a Text + title) in a Timeline.
   - Please Note: It helps to drag the Glow Effect onto a video clip in a Timeline that has natural lights in it such as a night shot with a car's headlights on.
2. Inspector > Effects > Glow > Set the Gain slider to maximum.
3. Inspector > Effects > Glow > Set the Horizontal/Vertical (H/V) slider all the way to the right.
4. Inspector > Effects > Glow > Set the Spread slider to maximum.
5. Inspector > Effects > Glow > You can keyframe the Shine Threshold to simulate a moving lens flare if you want.
6. Inspector > Effects > Glow > Set Color Filter to Blue, Pink, Orange, or White.
7. Inspector > Effects > Glow > Set Glow Framing to Vignette.

MIRRORS

The Mirrors Effect in DaVinci Resolve doubles a part of a video clip (or a Text + title) from one side of a dividing line to the other, and it creates an astonishing image of symmetry. Its perfect symmetry, in fact, can be remarkably compelling and mesmerizing. The Mirrors Effect can be used either vertically or horizontally. You can use the Mirrors Effect in DaVinci Resolve this way.

1. Effects > Open FX > Resolve FX Stylize > Drag the Mirrors Effect on top of a video clip (or a Text + title) in a Timeline.
2. Inspector > Effects > Mirrors Effect > Adjust the Angle used to create a symmetrical composition vertically or horizontally (Figure 85).

- An Angle of -90 degrees centers the dividing line horizontally.

KALEIDOSCOPE

The Kaleidoscope Effect in DaVinci Resolve divides a video clip (or a Text + title) into several overlapping and angular sections that interact with each other with mathematical precision. You can use the Kaleidoscope Effect in DaVinci Resolve this way.

1. Effects > Open FX > Resolve FX Stylize > Drag the Mirrors Effect on top of a video clip (or a Text + title) in a Timeline.
2. Inspector > Effects > Mirrors Effect > Mirror Placement > Kaleidoscope (Figure 86).
3. Inspector > Effects > Mirrors Effect > Adjust the Kaleidoscope's Position, Center Size, Angle, and Number of Sides, if needed.
   - Pro Tip: These parameters can be keyframed for even more control.

Figure 85: Mirrors Effect

Figure 86: Kaleidoscope Effect

INVERT COLOR

The Invert Color Effect in DaVinci Resolve produces some of the strongest visual imagery available on the computer today (with the computer's millions or billions of colors). It creates a negative of a video clip, and the colors that result from it can be surprisingly bold and unusual. You can use the Invert Color Effect in DaVinci Resolve this way.

1. Effects > Open FX > Resolve FX Color > Drag the Invert Color Effect on top of a video clip in a Timeline.
2. Inspector > Effects > Invert Color Effect > Adjust the Invert Color Effect's Invert Red, Invert Green, or Invert Blue parameters, if needed (Figure 87).
   - Pro Tip: Further Effects can be applied to a video clip with the Invert Color Effect applied to it for even more disarming imagery.

GAUSSIAN BLUR

The Gaussian Blur Effect in DaVinci Resolve can be used for blurring a video clip in the background when a Title is added on top. It can be used for creating a faux

DoF blurry background effect with a mask (and with a mask that even moves). It can be used for creating a blur-in transition (similar to a fade-in transition) and a blur-out transition as well. You can use the Gaussian Blur Effect in DaVinci Resolve this way.

1. Effects > Open FX > Resolve FX Blur > Drag the Gaussian Blur Effect on top of a video clip in a Timeline.
2. Inspector > Effects > Gaussian Blur Effect > Adjust the Gaussian Blur Effect's parameters.
    *   Pro Tip: Keyframes can be added to the Gaussian Blur Effect to provide full control over when the Gaussian Blur Effect occurs and how intensely it appears.

Figure 87: Invert Color Effect   Figure 88: Vignette

VIGNETTE

A Vignette on a video clip darkens and/or blurs the corners of a video clip's frame. It creates a sense of volume (i.e., depth) in an otherwise flat image. Some professional colorists put a small vignette on every single video clip in a movie. Vignettes can look very good – they add a painterly richness to a video clip – and they are rarely even noticed by audiences. The rule about a Vignette is "Make sure it doesn't look like a Vignette." A Vignette should look natural and never be noticeable. You can use the Vignette Effect in DaVinci Resolve this way.

1. Effects > Open FX > Resolve FX Stylize > Drag the Vignette Effect on top of a video clip in a Timeline.
2. Inspector > Effects > Vignette > Adjust the parameters of the Vignette Effect (Figure 88).
    A. Size slider.
    B. Anamorphism slider.
    C. Softness slider.
    D. Color.
        *   Pro Tip: You can also drag the Vignette Effect on top of an Adjustment Clip (on track 2) in a Timeline to affect multiple

video clips below it. Lengthen the Adjustment Clip over several video clips by dragging its end.

DOUBLE EXPOSURE

Creating a Double Exposure look on a video clip in a Timeline in DaVinci Resolve can look extremely professional, creative, and daring. You can create a Double Exposure look on a video clip in a Timeline in DaVinci Resolve this way.

1. Drag a video clip on a track above of the other video clips in a Timeline.
2. Select the video clip on the track above.
3. Inspector > Video > Composite > Drag the Opacity slider to about 50% or so to create a Double Exposure look.
   - Pro Tip: You can change the Composite Mode (i.e., Blend Mode) of the video clip on a track above the other video clips for even further effects.
     - Inspector > Video > Composite > Composite Mode > Select a Composite Mode other than Normal.
       - Pro Tip: You can quickly cycle through all the different Composite Modes in DaVinci Resolve by first hovering the mouse cursor over another Composite Mode and then pressing the up or down Arrow Keys on the keyboard.

ALPHA CHANNELS

If a video clip with an alpha channel (i.e., a transparent background) is not displaying its transparent background correctly in DaVinci Resolve, you can instruct DaVinci Resolve to use a different Alpha Channel Mode to display it with. (Free video clips with transparent backgrounds [and alpha channels] can be searched for and downloaded from the internet, and you can create your own graphics in video clips with transparent backgrounds in DaVinci Resolve. Graphics with transparent backgrounds typically look good placed above other video clips [on track 2] in a Timeline.)

- Right-click a video clip with a transparent background in a Timeline > Clip Attributes > Video > Alpha Mode > Select None or Premultiplied to adjust a video clip's transparent background display.

———

KEYFRAMES

———

Keyframes are control points added to video clips, audio clips, Transform Controls or Effects in DaVinci Resolve. They allow an editor to control editing decisions with mathematical precision and great finesse. They are applied to the "start" and "end" points of features in DaVinci Resolve, and their transitions ("animation curves") can simulate perfectly natural movement or stylized, mechanical movement. They are indispensable for serious editors, and DaVinci Resolve's keyframe controls are perhaps the easiest to use, and most neatly organized, in the entire video editing industry.

KEYFRAME A VIDEO CLIP
You can add a keyframe to a video clip in a Timeline in DaVinci Resolve this way.
1. Position the playhead over a video clip in a Timeline in DaVinci Resolve's Edit workspace where you want to create a "start" keyframe.
2. Inspector > Video > Click the diamond-shaped keyframe icon at the end of any parameter listed.
    • The diamond-shaped keyframe icon at the end of a parameter will turn red when activated (Figure 89).
3. Reposition the playhead in the Timeline over the video clip where you want to create an "end" keyframe.
4. Inspector > Video > Change the same parameter that you previously added a keyframe to.
    • A new keyframe will be automatically added to the parameter's new setting.
        • Pro Tip: Second keyframes are added automatically in DaVinci Resolve whenever you move the playhead in a Timeline and adjust a parameter that you have previously set a keyframe to. Why? To make it easier to apply

keyframes when you have a lot of keyframes to apply. If this seems confusing, since it is so unintuitive, you can always add the second keyframe manually in the same way that you added the first keyframe. Just click the diamond-shaped keyframe icon at the end of the parameter you previously set a keyframe to (so it will turn red) and then adjust the parameter's setting.

- Pro Tip: You can view the keyframes added to a video clip in a Timeline by clicking the diamond-shaped keyframe icon at the bottom right corner of a video clip. A small blue track will appear below the video clip, and the white diamonds on it are keyframes. The keyframes here can be dragged to different positions.

Figure 89: Red Diamond Keyframe

Figure 90: Keyframe Interpolation (Linear/Ease)

NAVIGATE KEYFRAMES

You can navigate to the previous or next keyframe on a video clip in a Timeline in DaVinci Resolve this way.

1. Select a video clip in a Timeline that has multiple keyframes applied to it.
2. Inspector > Video > Click the Previous or Next Arrows flanking the diamond-shaped keyframe icon at the end of a parameter that has multiple keyframes applied to it.
   - The Previous Arrow moves the playhead above the previous keyframe.
   - The Next Arrow moves the playhead above the next keyframe.
     - When the playhead is exactly on top of a keyframe, the diamond-shaped keyframe icon in the Inspector will turn red.

REMOVE A KEYFRAME

You can remove a keyframe from a video clip in a Timeline in DaVinci Resolve this way.

1. Select a video clip in a Timeline that has multiple keyframes applied to it.
2. Inspector > Video > Click the Previous or Next Arrows flanking the diamond-shaped keyframe icon at the end of a parameter to move the playhead exactly on top of a keyframe. It will turn red.
3. Click the red diamond-shaped keyframe icon at the end of the parameter.
    *   It will turn blank. This means that its keyframe has been removed.

DELETE ALL KEYFRAMES

You can delete all keyframes from a video clip in a Timeline in DaVinci Resolve this way.

1. Select a video clip in a Timeline that has multiple keyframes applied to it.
2. Inspector > Video > Click the Reset icon (the half circle arrow) at the end of a parameter that has keyframes.
    *   All of the keyframes on the parameter will be reset to none (i.e., removed).

KEYFRAME INTERPOLATIONS

The transition between keyframes on a video clip, an audio clip, the Transport controls, or an Effect in DaVinci Resolve is called an "interpolation." An interpolation produces an "animation curve." It controls whether the transition to the next keyframe is abrupt (with a Linear keyframe), slow to start (with an Ease In keyframe), slow to end (with an Ease Out keyframe), or both slow to start and slow to end (with a Both keyframe). These keyframe types can create curvy lines (i.e., smooth Bezier lines) that gently connect the different keyframes or straight lines (i.e., linear lines) that abruptly connect the keyframes. You can change the "interpolation" of a keyframe in DaVinci Resolve this way.

1. Select a video clip in a Timeline that has multiple keyframes applied to it.
2. Inspector > Video > Click the Previous or Next Arrows flanking the diamond-shaped keyframe icon at the end of a parameter to move the playhead exactly on top of a keyframe.
3. Inspector > Video > Right-click the red diamond-shaped icon at the end of a parameter > Select one of the following keyframe (interpolation) types available (Figure 90):
    *   Linear = abrupt start and abrupt end.
    *   Ease In = slow start.
    *   Ease Out = slow end.
    *   Ease In and Out = slow start and slow end.

KEYFRAME EDITOR

The Keyframe Editor in DaVinci Resolve's Edit workspace allows keyframes to be "edited" with greater control than they can be edited in the Inspector. The

Keyframe Editor resides below a video clip in a Timeline, and it can be opened or closed at any time by clicking the diamond-shaped keyframe icon at the bottom right corner of a video clip. At least one keyframe must always be applied to a video clip in the Inspector first before the Keyframe Editor will be available in a Timeline. You can access the Keyframe Editor in DaVinci Resolve this way.

- Click the diamond-shaped keyframe icon at the bottom right corner of a video clip in a Timeline that has keyframes on it.
  - or Clip > Show Keyframe Editor
    - The white diamond shapes in the Keyframe Editor are keyframes. They can be dragged to new locations (Figure 91).
    - Keyframe Tracks appear as rows for different parameters such as Transform, Composite, or Opacity, etc. Each different parameter (containing keyframes) will appear as separate tracks.
    - Keyframe Sub-tracks appear as rows inside of rows. These rows contain further video clip parameters such as Zoom, Position, or Rotate, etc (Figure 92).
      - You can expand a Keyframe Sub-track on the Keyframe Editor by clicking its disclosure triangle at the end of its row.

Figure 91: Keyframe Editor   Figure 92: Keyframe Sub-tracks

KEYFRAME EDITOR'S FUNCTIONS

The following functions are available in the Keyframe Editor in DaVinci Resolve:

1. Add a Keyframe.
   - Option-click a Keyframe Track.
2. Copy a Keyframe.
   - Option-drag a keyframe. (Option-dragging creates a copy of an item automatically.)
     - or Select a keyframe, press Command C, reposition the playhead, and press Command V.
3. Convert a Keyframe's Type.
   - Right-click a Keyframe > Select one of the keyframe types:

- Linear = abrupt start and abrupt end.
- Ease In = slow start.
- Ease Out = slow end.
- Ease In and Out = slow start and slow end.

4.   Select Multiple Keyframes.
- Marquee drag over multiple keyframes.
- or Command-click non-contiguous keyframes.

5.   Move a Keyframe.
- Drag a keyframe left or right.
- A Tool Tip appears and reveals the number of frames the keyframed has been dragged.

6.   Delete a Keyframe.
   A.   Select a keyframe.
   B.   Press delete.

CURVE EDITOR

The Curve Editor in DaVinci Resolve's Edit workspace allows the animation "curves lines" between keyframes to be changed from Linear to Bezier (i.e., from straight lines to curvy lines). It can produce either abrupt movement or smooth movement and it can look mechanical or natural. The Curve Editor opens up below a video clip in a Timeline of the Edit workspace that has keyframes on it. At least one keyframe must always be added to a video clip in the Inspector first before the Curve Editor will be available in a Timeline. You can open up the Curve Editor in DaVinci Resolve's Edit workspace this way.

- Click the icon with a curvy line between two diamond-shaped keyframes at the bottom right corner of a video clip in a Timeline (Figure 93).
- or Clip > Show Curve Editor

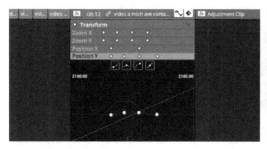

Figure 93: Curve Editor   Figure 94: Keyframe Handle

CURVE EDITOR'S FUNCTIONS

The following functions are available in the Curve Editor in DaVinci Resolve:

1. Select or Disable Parameters with Keyframes on them to focus on only one parameter at a time.
   - Click a parameter listed in the drop down menu located in the top left corner of the Curve Editor.
     - This is a good way to temporarily hide multiple parameters with keyframes on them and create a less distracting environment to work in.
2. Add a keyframe.
   - Option-click an animation curve line.
3. Copy a Keyframe.
   - Option-drag a keyframe. (Option-dragging creates a copy of an item automatically.)
     - or Select a keyframe, press Command C, reposition the playhead, and press Command V.
4. Convert a keyframe type.
   A. Select a keyframe.
   B. Click a keyframe type button at the top of the Curve Editor:
      - Ease In = slow start.
      - Both = slow start and slow end.
      - Ease Out = slow end.
      - Linear = abrupt start and abrupt end.
5. Reshape a Bezier animation curve line manually.
   A. Select a Bezier keyframe (i.e., an Ease In, Ease Out, or Both keyframe) in the Curve Editor
      - It turns red and its curve handles appear.
   B. Pull a curve handle to manually reshape the animation curve line underneath the keyframe.
      - Pro Tip: You can convert a keyframe's handle tangent by Command-dragging a keyframe's handle for even more control (Figure 94).
6. Change the timing (position) of a keyframe.
   - Drag a keyframe left or right. A Tool Tip shows the position and value change.
     - Pro Tip: Shift-dragging a keyframe left or right moves the keyframe in a straight line so that its value (amount) will not be altered.
7. Change the value (amount) of a keyframe.
   - Drag a keyframe up or down. A Tool Tip shows the position and value change.
     - Pro Tip: Shift-dragging a keyframe up or down moves it in a straight line so that its timing (position) will not be altered.

8. Delete a Keyframe.
    A. Select a keyframe.
    B. Press delete.

_____

AUDIO

DaVinci Resolve's Edit workspace has substantial audio controls for enhancing the sound of video and audio clips, and it has professional Audio Effects to apply to video and audio clips for creative manipulation as well. The Fairlight workspace of DaVinci Resolve is a full-fledged digital audio workstation (DAW), in addition, with professional audio engineering and mastering capabilities. Using the audio controls in DaVinci Resolve's Edit workspace is the main focus of this chapter; however, there are a few explanations of the audio capabilities of DaVinci Resolve's Fairlight workspace provided as well.

AUDIO CLIP INFORMATION
A video or audio clip's metadata (i.e., information), such as sample rate or bit depth, can be found in DaVinci Resolve's Metadata panel here.
- Right-click a video or audio clip in the Media Pool or Timeline > Metadata
  - *Metadata* is located near the word *Inspector* in the DaVinci Resolve user interface. Click the word *Metadata* to open up the full Metadata panel and see a video or audio clip's full information.

AUDIO CHANNELS
The audio channels of a video or audio clip can be found in the Clip Attributes feature in the Media Pool or Timeline in DaVinci Resolve.
- Right-click a video or audio clip in the Media Pool or Timeline in DaVinci Resolve > Clip Attributes > Audio > Format, Tracks and Channel in Track.

AUDIO TRACK CHANNELS
The top right corner of an audio track's header in a Timeline indicates an audio track's channels (Figure 95).
- 1.0 = mono (one channel).

- 2.0 = stereo (two channels).
- 5.1 = surround (five channels plus a sub woofer).

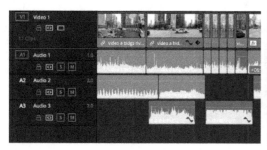
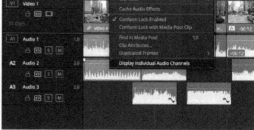

Figure 95: Mono (1.0)/Stereo (2.0)   Figure 96: Display Individual Audio Channels

DISPLAY OPTIONS (FOR AUDIO CHANNELS)
You can display the audio channels inside an audio clip in a Timeline in DaVinci Resolve this way.
- Right-click an audio clip in a Timeline > Display Individual Audio Channels (Figure 96).
  - In the Edit workspace, the individual audio channels can be displayed only.
  - In the Fairlight workspace, the audio channels can be displayed and edited individually.

CHANGE AUDIO TRACK CHANNELS
You can change an audio track's channels in DaVinci Resolve this way.
- Right-click an audio track's header in a Timeline > Change Track Type To > Mono, Stereo, or 5.1 (Figure 97).

CONVERT STEREO TO MONO
You can convert an audio track's stereo channels to mono in DaVinci Resolve this way.
- Right-click an audio clip in the Media Pool or a Timeline > Clip Attributes > Audio > Source Channel > Change Embed Channel 2 to Embed Channel 1.
  - This interleaves the two stereo channels of the audio into one mono channel, and the same signal plays out through both the left and right channels.

DISPLAY OPTIONS (FOR AUDIO TRACKS)
You can display an audio track in a Timeline in DaVinci Resolve in 3 different ways.

Figure 97: Change to Mono/Stereo   Figure 98: Show Full Clip Audio Waveform

- Click the Timeline View Options icon in the top left corner of a Timeline >
  Audio View Options
    A. Non-Rectified Waveform = shows an audio waveform from the
        bottom up.
    B. Full Waveform = shows the top and bottom parts of an audio wave-
        form.
    C. Waveform Border = adds a border to an audio waveform so it be
        seen more clearly.

RENAME AN AUDIO TRACK
You can rename an audio track in DaVinci Resolve this way.
1. Click the name of an audio track on an audio track's header in a Timeline.
2. Type in a new name.
    - Pro Tip: DIA for dialog, SFX for sound effects, and MUS for music
      are common names for audio tracks used by experienced filmmakers.

AUDIO TRACK COLOR
You can change an audio track's color in DaVinci Resolve this way.
- Right-click an audio track header in a Timeline > Change Track Color >
  Color

SHOW AUDIO WAVEFORM (IN SOURCE VIEWER)
You can open up a video clip or an audio clip in the Source Viewer of DaVinci Resolve in order to see its audio waveform. This is useful for precisely selecting a section of a video or audio clip instead of selecting an entire video or audio clip. You
can add *in* (I) and *out* (O) points around the transients (high peaks) of the audio
waveform of a video or audio clip and then drag the section into a Timeline. It
makes the process of editing selections from video or audio clips very precise. You
can show the audio waveform of a video or audio clip in the Source Viewer in
DaVinci Resolve this way.

1. Double click an audio clip in the Media Pool to open it up in the Source Viewer.
2. Double click a video clip in the Media Pool to open it up in the Source Viewer > . . . (Options) drop down menu > Show Full Clip Audio Waveform (Figure 98).
   - You can add *in* (I) and *out* (O) points around the transients (high peaks) of an audio waveform that you want by pressing the I and O keys on the keyboard, and then drag the portion (or section) of the clip into a Timeline.

ADJUST VOLUME

You can adjust the volume of a video or audio clip in a Timeline in DaVinci Resolve in three different ways.
- Select a video or audio clip in a Timeline.
   1. Inspector > Audio > Adjust the Volume slider (Figure 99).
   2. Drag the Volume Line on top of a video or audio clip in a Timeline up or down (Figure 100).
      - You may have to zoom in first to see the Volume Line clearly.
   3. Keyboard Shortcuts:
      - Option-Command + increases the volume 1 dB.
      - Option-Command - decreases the volume 1 dB.

Figure 99: Inspector > Volume Slider   Figure 100: Volume Line

KEYFRAME VOLUME LINE

One of the easiest ways to level out the loud parts of a video clip or an audio clip in a Timeline in DaVinci Resolve, and to level up the quiet parts as well, is with keyframes on its Volume Line. This requires using 4 separate keyframes in a group.
   1. First, zoom in to see the Volume Line on a video or audio clip in a Timeline.
      - You may have to drag the dividing line on top of the audio tracks up to provide more room to see the audio tracks clearly.

2. Drag the dividing line at the bottom of an audio track header down to increase the height of an audio track and see its audio waveform better.
3. Option-click the Volume Line at the "start" of a loud section of an audio waveform.
   - This creates keyframe 1. It is shown as a red or white diamond on the Volume Line.
4. Option-click the Volume Line again but away from keyframe 1.
   - This creates keyframe 2.
5. Option-click the Volume Line at the "end" of the loud section of the audio waveform.
   - This creates keyframe 3.
6. Option-click the Volume Line again but away from keyframe 3.
   - This creates keyframe 4.
7. Now that 4 keyframes in a group have been set on the Volume Line, drag the part of the Volume Line between the two innermost keyframes down to lower the volume of the loud part (Figure 101).
   - The outer two keyframes remain the same to maintain the volume level of the rest of the audio track.
8. Repeat this technique of using 4 keyframes in a group on all loud parts, and to raise the volume of all quiet parts on the Volume Line.

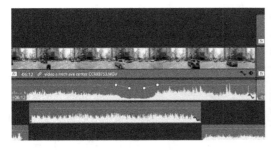

Figure 101: Keyframed Volume Line   Figure 102: Fade In and Out

FADE AUDIO IN / OUT

Most audio clips should have a fade in and a fade out in order to sound professional and natural. If they do not have a fade in or out, they can sound abrupt or jarring. You can add a fade in or fade out to an audio clip in a Timeline in DaVinci Resolve this way.

1. Hover the mouse cursor over an audio clip in a Timeline.
2. Drag the white boxes that appear in the top left and right corners of the audio clip inward (Figure 102).
   - This creates a fade in or fade out.

- A Tool Tip shows how many frames have been dragged inward to let you create a short or long fade.

PANNING

You can pan an audio clip left or right in DaVinci Resolve this way.

1. Select an audio clip in a Timeline.
2. Inspector > Audio > Adjust the Pan slider.
   - Pro Tip: The Pan slider can be keyframed to create the famous panning effect used in the Sergeant Pepper album from The Beatles. This effect makes the sound from the left channel gradually move to the right channel and back again, over a long period of time. It can be heard best on headphones.

ADD VIDEO ONLY

You can add only a video's clip's video portion from the Source Viewer to a Timeline in DaVinci Resolve this way.

1. Double click a video clip in the Media Pool to open it up in the Source Viewer.
2. Click the Video Only (Filmstrip) icon that appears at the bottom of the Source Viewer and drag it to a Timeline.
   - Pro Tip: You can manually delete the audio portion of a video clip and keep just the video portion: add the video clip to a Timeline, detach its video portion from the audio portion by clicking the chain icon at the top of the Timeline toolbar, select the audio track alone, and press delete. The audio portion will disappear and the video portion will remain.

ADD AUDIO ONLY

You can add only a video's clip's audio portion from the Source Viewer to a Timeline in DaVinci Resolve this way.

1. Double click a video clip in the Media Pool to open it up in the Source Viewer.
2. Click the Audio Only (Waveform) icon that appears at the bottom of the Source Viewer and drag it to a Timeline.
   - Pro Tip: You can manually delete the video portion of a video clip and keep just the audio portion: add the video clip to a Timeline, detach its audio portion from the video portion by clicking the chain icon at the top of the Timeline toolbar, select the video track alone, and press delete. The video portion will disappear and the audio portion will remain.

DELETE AUDIO FROM A VIDEO

You can delete the audio portion of a video clip in a Timeline in DaVinci Resolve this way.

1. Select a video clip in a Timeline.
2. Click the chain link icon in the Timeline toolbar.
   - or Right click the video clip > Link Clips (Figure 103)
3. Select the audio portion of the video clip.
4. Press delete.

Figure 103: Detach (Unlink) Audio   Figure 104: Audio Meters (in Audio Mixer)

AUDIO MIXER

You can open the Audio Mixer in DaVinci Resolve this way.

- Click the word *Mixer* located near the word *Metadata* or *Inspector* in the top right corner of the DaVinci Resolve user interface.
  - Pro Tip: The Audio Mixer in DaVinci Resolve's Edit workspace has the following features:
    - Channel Strips = correspond to each audio track in a Timeline, named Audio 1, Audio 2 , and Audio 3, for example.
    - S = Solo an audio track.
    - M = Mute an audio track.
    - EQ = opens up the Equalizer.

AUDIO METERS

The Audio Meters in DaVinci Resolve's Edit workspace show the volume levels of each audio track in a Timeline. They provide a visual gauge of how loud or quiet an audio track is, and they can be useful for mixing the volume levels of different audio tracks together. The audio levels (volume levels) of an audio track should be roughly between -15 dB and -3 dB on the Audio Meters. Any level above 0 dB on the audio meters will produce distortion (caused by clipping). You can reveal the Audio Meters in DaVinci Resolve this way.

- Audio Mixer > . . . (Options) drop down menu > Meters (Figure 104)
  - or Workspace Menu > Show Panel in Workspace > Meters

SYNCHRONIZE AUDIO

Double-system sound (i.e., video recorded in a camera with an external microphone on an external recorder) is the best way to get professional sounding audio in a video. However, an external audio recording must also be synchronized to the audio that was recorded on the camera's video file later on (known as a "scratch track") to work. Single-system sound, by contrast (such as a video recorded on a cell phone), is produced by both a camera lens and a microphone located inside the cell phone itself. The camera and microphone are located together in a cell phone, which means that there is never any need to synchronize an audio file, recorded externally, to the video file. You can synchronize audio recordings made from an external microphone on an external recorder to a video clips' internal audio recording (scratch track) in DaVinci Resolve this way.

1. Select both the external audio recording files (from an external recorder) and the video recording files from a camera in the Media Pool.
2. Right-click any of them > Auto Sync Audio > Based on Waveform (Figure 105).
    - The video clips will have the appropriate external audio recording files attached to them automatically in synchronization.
        - Pro Tip: It helps to use a Clapper Board in front of a camera lens before recording a double-system sound video. Clapping your hands twice in front of a camera lens as well, if you don't have a Clapper Board, can work well. DaVinci Resolve can sync-up the Clapper Board or the two hand claps on a video and its corresponding audio file much more effectively than a video or audio file without a Clapper Board or a hand clap.

Figure 105: Sync Audio

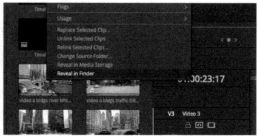

Figure 106: Reveal Audio Clip (in Finder)

REVEAL A SYNCED AUDIO CLIP

You can reveal a synchronized audio clip on a computer (in case it goes missing) in DaVinci Resolve this way.

- Right-click a video clip in a Timeline > Reveal Synced Audio in Media Pool.
    - Pro Tip: You can find the audio clip on a computer's hard drive as well.
        - Right-click the Synced Audio clip in the Media Pool > Reveal in Finder (Figure 106).

RELINK MISSING AUDIO FILES

A large red image may be seen in the DaVinci Resolve user interface whenever a video or audio file has gone missing. This usually happens when a video or audio file has been moved to a different external drive or when a video or audio file has been renamed. You can relink missing video or audio files in DaVinci resolve this way.

1. Edit Page > Media Pool > Click the Relink Media icon at the top of the Media Pool.
2. Click the Locate button in the dialog box that appears and browse for the approximate folder that your video or audio clips were originally in.
3. Select the folder on your hard drive where your video or audio clips were originally placed.
4. DaVinci Resolve will scan all the video and audio clips inside the folder and automatically relink the missing ones in the Media Pool.
    - Alternatively, you can select the Disk Search button in the dialog box to have DaVinci Resolve search an entire hard drive on a computer, but be prepared for this to take a lot of time.
        - Pro Tip: If the steps above don't work, you can manually search for the original video or audio clips on your computer and just re-import them into your Media Pool a second time.

NUDGE AN AUDIO CLIP

You may need to nudge an audio clip in order to correct an out-of-sync playback issue or to adjust an audio edit creatively.

1. Select a video clip in a Timeline
2. Click the chain link icon in the Timeline toolbar to unlink (i.e., detach) the audio portion of the video clip.
3. Turn Snapping off.
4. Select the audio portion of the video clip.
5. Use keyframe shortcuts to nudge the detached audio clip.
    - Comma nudges an audio clip left one frame at a time.
    - Period nudges an audio clip right one frame at a time.

SUBFRAME AUDIO EDITING

DaVinci Resolve allows users to edit audio clips down to the subframe (i.e., sample) level at which an audio track was originally recorded. This must be done, however, in the Fairlight workspace of DaVinci Resolve because it is not available in the Edit workspace. The Edit workspace zooms in on an audio waveform at just the frame level of a video clip which is usually 24 or 30 frames per second. The Fairlight workspace zooms in on an audio waveform all the way to the subframe level (i.e., the sample level) at which an audio clip was originally recoded. Subframe audio editing allows users to correct pops or glitches in an audio waveform and redraw its samples manually. You can edit an audio clip on the subframe level in DaVinci Resolve this way (Figure 107).

1. DaVinci Resolve Menu > Preferences > User > Editing > Make sure Align Audio Edits to Frame Boundaries is unchecked (it may be already off by default).
2. Select an audio clip in a Timeline of DaVinci Resolve's Edit workspace.
3. Move to the Fairlight (DAW) workspace.
   - Click the Fairlight icon at the bottom of the DaVinci Resolve user interface.
4. In the Fairlight workspace, select the audio clip.
5. Turn Snapping off.
6. Zoom in to where a pop or a glitch can be seen visually on the audio clip's waveform.
7. Redraw the samples over the pop or the glitch (i.e., the spikes) in the audio clip's waveform (Figure 108).
   - Hold the mouse cursor down on a sample that is at the correct volume level in the waveform before the pop or glitch and manually drag it over the pop or glitch to a sample at the correct volume level on the other side of the pop or glitch.
     - This manually "redraws" the samples in the waveform over the pop or glitch to remove the spikes from the waveform.
8. Return to the Edit workspace.
   - Click the Edit icon at the bottom of the DaVinci Resolve user interface.
9. Turn the subframe editing option back on in DaVinci Resolve's user preferences (unless it was originally off by default).
   - DaVinci Resolve Menu > Preferences > User > Editing > Recheck Align Audio Edits to Frame Boundaries back on again.

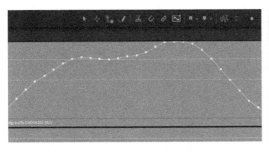

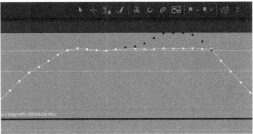

Figure 107: Subframe Audio (Glitch)   Figure 108: Subframe Audio (Glitch Redrawn)

ADD AN AUDIO EFFECT

Reverb, Delay, Chorus, Echo, Noise Reduction, and Distortion are some of the prominent Audio Effects that can be added to a video or audio clip in DaVinci Resolve, and there are many more audio effects available. Their parameters can be adjusted in the Inspector with keyframes to provide full control over when they occur and how intensely they sound. You can add an Audio Effect to a video or audio clip in DaVinci Resolve this way.

1. Effects > Audio FX > Drag an Audio Effect on top of the audio portion of a video clip or on top of an audio clip in a Timeline (Figure 109).
2. Inspector > Effects > Audio Effect Name > Adjust the Audio Effect's parameters.

Figure 109: Audio Effects   Figure 110: Full Audio Panel

FULL AUDIO CONTROLS PANEL

You can open an Audio Effect's full controls panel in DaVinci Resolve this way.

- Inspector > Effects > Audio Effect Name > Click the 3-lines icon on the Audio Effect's title bar to open up its full controls panel.
    - A large panel of the Audio Effect's full controls will appear for much easier access and use (Figure 110).

DEACTIVATE AN AUDIO EFFECT
You can deactivate an Audio Effect in DaVinci Resolve this way.
- Inspector > Effects > Audio Effect Name > Click the red dot next to an Audio Effect's title so that it turns gray (deactivated).

REMOVE AN AUDIO EFFECT
You can remove an Audio Effect in DaVinci Resolve this way.
- Inspector > Effects > Audio Effect Name > Click the trash can icon next to an Audio Effect's title.

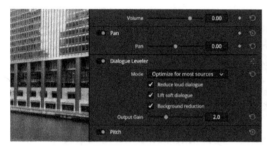

Figure 111: Dialog Leveler (in Inspector)   Figure 112: Dialog Processor (in Audio FX)

NOISE REDUCTION
DaVinci Resolve's Edit workspace has several Noise Reduction features that can help clean up a video clip's audio track or an audio clip itself. They work especially well on audio clips containing dialog. These Noise Reduction features are Dialog Leveler, Dialog Processor, Noise Reduction, and Vocal Channel. The Equalizer in the Inspector, as well, can be used to clean up audio. DaVinci Resolve's Fairlight (DAW) workspace has even more Noise Reduction features that can help clean up audio.

1. Dialog Leveler
   A. First, select a video clip with an audio track or an audio clip in a Timeline.
   B. Inspector > Audio > Dialog Leveler > Adjust its parameters > Reduce Loud Dialog, Lift Soft Dialog, Background Reduction, and Output Gain (Figure 111)
      - Pro Tip: You can toggle the parameters of the Dialog Leveler on or off by clicking the red dot next to each one in order to hear how each one sounds.
2. Dialog Processor
   A. Effects > Audio FX > Drag the Dialog Processor Effect on top of the audio portion of a video clip or an audio clip in a Timeline (Figure 112).

    B.   Inspector > Effects > Dialog Processor > Adjust its parameters > De-Rumble, De-Pop, De-Ess, Compressor, Expander, Excite
- Pro Tip: All dials can be reset to unity (default) by double-clicking them.
- Pro Tip: You can toggle the parameters of the Dialog Processor Effect on or off by clicking the red dot next to each one in order to hear how each one sounds.
- Pro Tip: You can open up the Dialog Processor Effect's full controls panel by clicking the 3-lines icon on the Dialog Processor Effect's title bar in the Inspector.

3.   Noise Reduction
    A.   Effects > Audio FX > Drag the Noise Reduction Effect on top of the audio portion of a video clip or an audio clip in a Timeline.
    B.   Inspector > Effects > Noise Reduction > Adjust its parameters > Detection, Smoothing, Output (Figure 113)
- Pro Tip: The presets drop down menu items of De-Hiss, De-Rumble, and De-Rumble and Hiss work well as starting points.
- Pro Tip: All dials can be reset to unity (default) by double-clicking them.
- Pro Tip: You can toggle the parameters of the Noise Reduction Effect on or off by clicking the red dot next to each one in order to hear how each one sounds.
- Pro Tip: You can open up the Noise Reduction Effect's full controls panel by clicking the 3-lines icon on the Noise Reduction Effect's title bar in the Inspector.

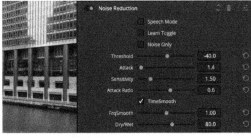

Figure 113: Noise Reduction   Figure 114: Vocal Channel

4.   Vocal Channel
    A.   Effects > Audio FX > Drag the Vocal Channel Effect on top of the audio portion of a video clip or an audio clip in a Timeline.

    B.   Inspector > Effects > Vocal Channel > Adjust its parameters > High Pass, Equalizer, and Compressor (Figure 114)
- Pro Tip: All dials can be reset to unity (default) by double-clicking them.
- Pro Tip: You can toggle the parameters of the Vocal Channel Effect on or off by clicking the red dot next to each one in order to hear how each one sounds.
- Pro Tip: You can open up the Vocal Channel Effect's full controls panel by clicking the 3-lines icon on the Vocal Channel Effect's title bar in the Inspector.

EQUALIZER

The Equalizer in DaVinci Resolve's Edit workspace "equalizes" the different frequencies (i.e., pitches) of sound in an audio clip. It can increase or decrease the bass, the midrange, or the treble sounds of an audio clip by dragging the line on top of the Equalizer's graph up or down. It can remove the low end rumble (such as room tone) of an audio clip by rolling off the low end section of the Equalizer, and it can remove the high end hiss that is not needed in an audio clip by rolling off the high end section of the Equalizer. You can use the Equalizer in DaVinci Resolve this way.

1. Select a video or audio clip in a Timeline.
2. Inspector > Audio > Equalizer.
3. Select and then drag the different bands (i.e., sections) of the line on top of the Equalizer's graph up or down to produce a change in pitch.
   - Pro Tip: Drag the lowest band (band 1) down to remove the unwanted hum, rumble, or room tone in an audio clip.
   - Pro Tip: Drag the highest band (band 4) down to remove the unwanted hiss in an audio clip.

NORMALIZE AUDIO

Normalizing audio in DaVinci Resolve's Edit workspace involves changing an audio clip's loudest part to a preset standard level. This is a quick and easy way of adjusting (or "normalizing") the volume level of an audio clip or several audio clips at once. You can Normalize an audio clip in DaVinci Resolve this way.

1. Right click an audio clip (or several audio clips) in a Timeline > Normalize Audio Levels.
       A.   Normalization Mode > Sample Peak Program (Figure 115)
       B.   Target Level: -3.0 dBFS
   - Pro Tip: You can select one of the professional target presets listed (i.e., LUFS presets) in the Normalize dialog box. (You-

Tube's professional target LUFS setting, for example, is -14 dBFS.)

C. Set Level:
- Independent = select this for one clip.
- Relative = select this for multiple clips.

D. Click Normalize
- Pro Tip: You can watch the audio waveform of an audio clip in a Timeline change to the Normalization settings set when Normalization occurs.
- Pro Tip: Further volume settings can be applied after the Normalization process is used in DaVinci Resolve, which means that you can use Normalize as the first step of an audio clean-up workflow.

Figure 115: Normalize

Figure 116: Compressor (in Vocal Channel)

AUDIO COMPRESSOR

An Audio Compressor in DaVinci Resolve's Edit workspace "compresses" the loudest parts of an audio clip and raises the lowest parts up to even out its overall volume level. An Audio Compressor is typically used on audio clips that have both high volume levels and low volume levels and are somewhat difficult to manually even out with keyframes. You can use an Audio Compressor in DaVinci Resolve's Edit workspace this way.

1. Effects > Audio FX > Drag the Vocal Channel Effect on top of an audio clip in a Timeline.
2. Inspector > Effects > Vocal Channel Effect > Click the 3-lines icon on the Vocal Channel's title bar to open up the Vocal Channel Effect's full controls panel (Figure 116).
    A. Click the red dot on the Compressor section of the Vocal Channel's full controls panel to activate the Compressor.
        I.   Ratio = set this to 7 or so.
        II. Gain = set this to 12 or so.

- Experiment with different Ratio and Gain settings to hear what creates the most even sounding audio level.
- Pro Tip: All dials can be reset to unity (default) by double-clicking them.

Figure 117: Compressor (in Fairlight)

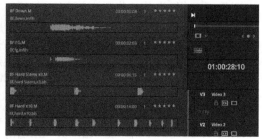

Figure 118: Foley Library

AUDIO COMPRESSOR (FAIRLIGHT)

You can use the Audio Compressor in DaVinci Resolve's Fairlight as well this way.

1. Select an audio clip in a Timeline of DaVinci Resolve's Edit workspace.
2. Switch to the Fairlight workspace.
   - Click the Fairlight workspace icon at the bottom of the DaVinci Resolve user interface.
3. Select the audio clip in Fairlight.
4. Show the Audio Mixer in Fairlight.
   - Click the word *Mixer* by the words *Meters*, *Metadata*, and *Inspector* at the top right corner of the Fairlight user interface.
5. In the Mixer that appears, double-click the Dynamics Graph on the Channel Strip that the audio clip is on.
   - The Dynamics full controls panel will open up (Figure 117).
     - A. Click the red dot next to the Compressor in the Dynamics' full controls panel to activate the Compressor.
     - B. Select one of the professional presets listed in the Presets drop down menu (such as Dialog Compression) to get started, or else manually set the controls listed below.
       - I. Threshold = set this to -10 or so.
       - II. Ratio = set this to 3:1 or 2:1.
       - III. Mix = set this to 0.
         - Experiment with different Threshold, Ratio, and Mix settings to hear what creates the most even sounding audio level.

FOLEY EFFECTS LIBRARY

DaVinci Resolve's free Foley Effects Library can be downloaded as additional download material and can be added to DaVinci Resolve very easily. It contains mostly Foley sound effects such as footsteps, body movements, and physical activities, but not general sound effects like wind, rain, or thunder, so it may not be useful for everyone. It is about 1 TB in size. You can download the free Foley Effects Library in DaVinci Resolve this way.

- DaVinci Resolve Menu > Additional Download Material > Foley Effects Library (Figure 118).
  - Pro Tip: Once installed, you can see all the Foley Effects listed in the Foley Effects Library in DaVinci Resolve by typing 3 asterisks (* * *) into its search bar.

———

EXPORT

———

Multiple export options and professional export presets are available in DaVinci Resolve's Deliver workspace. Data rate, audio, alpha channels, format, and a host of other items, can be adjusted during export, and multiple versions of a video can be exported together all at once. DaVinci Resolve's export options can even be customized for personal preference and saved for later reuse. (The "codecs," "formats," and "container formats" explained in the *Codecs* section of the *Media Management* chapter in *DaVinci Resolve Editing Step By Step Instructions* may be helpful for editors to read so that they will be able to better understand how to use the different export formats available in DaVinci Resolve's Deliver workspace.)

EXPORT A SELECTION

You can export a small section of a video instead of an entire video Timeline in DaVinci Resolve by adding *in* (I) and *out* (O) points around a section of a video and exporting that selection only. You can add *in* (I) and *out* (O) points around a section of a video Timeline in DaVinci Resolve this way.

1. Position the playhead over the "start" of a section of a video in a Timeline where you want to create an *in* point.
   - Press I.
2. Reposition the playhead over the "end" of a section of the video in the Timeline where you want to create an *out* point.
   - Press O.
     - These *in* and *out* points will appear at the top of the Timeline, and they can be dragged further for more refined positioning before exporting (Figure 119).
       - Pro Tip: You can delete the *in* and *out* points that you have created in a Timeline, if you have made a mis-

take, for example, and start over again by pressing Option X (or Mark Menu > Clear In and Out).

3. Export the video selection.
    • Use the Quick Export option (explained below) or the full Deliver workspace of DaVinci Resolve to export the video selection.

Figure 119: Export a Selection   Figure 120: Quick Export

QUICK EXPORT

The easiest way to export a video in DaVinci Resolve is with the Quick Export feature in the Edit Workspace. Quick Export provides the most practical and reliable export options available for most video editors. Quick Export exports 1080p videos, however, not 4K videos.

1. First, select the Timeline in DaVinci Resolve's Edit workspace by clicking inside the Timeline area.
    • or Select a section of an entire video Timeline that you want to export by setting *in* (I) and *out* (O) points around a section that you want (as explained in *Export A Section of A Video* above.)
2. File Menu > Quick Export (Figure 120)
3. Select a preset listed in the Quick Export dialog box:
    • H.264 Master = the most practical and reliable export preset for playing a video on the internet and for sharing in general.
    • ProRes or DNxHD = export formats for editing (as opposed to sharing). These create extremely large file sizes.
4. Click Export
5. Save As > Name the exported video.
6. Where > Desktop, or select another location on a computer.
7. Click Save.
    • A progress bar will appear to indicate how long the export process will take.

DATA RATES

The exported file size of a video is determined by its format, length, and data rate. The data rate of a video is also what determines its image quality. A low data rate setting will create a relatively low or weak image quality in a video, whereas a high data rate setting will create a high or strong image quality in a video. A high data rate setting is especially useful when color grading so that a computer can grab ahold of a video's pixels well and manipulate them fully. Nevertheless, there are no set standards for what a video's final data rate should be. The data rate of the original footage recorded by a camera should be known and the data rate required of a video's final destination should be known in order to use a data rate setting effectively. For professional filmmakers, a camera's highest data rate setting should be used when recording video footage and the same data rate setting should be used when exporting a final video unless other requirements intervene. Film festivals and streaming services require certain data rate settings, and they usually post their data rate settings online so that filmmakers can adjust their export settings accordingly. You can use the data rate settings in DaVinci Resolve to export a video this way.

1. First, select a Timeline in DaVinci Resolve's Edit workspace by clicking inside the Timeline area.
   - or Select a section of an entire video Timeline that you want to export by setting *in* (I) and *out* (O) points around a section that you want (as explained in *Export A Section of A Video* above.)
2. Deliver workspace > Custom Export > Codec > H264 > Quality > Restrict to > Type in the data rate that you want in Kb/s (Figure 121).
   - Pro Tip: You can find a video's actual data rate size in Mbps listed here.
     - Open up a video clip in Apple's Quicktime Player software > Window > Show Movie Inspector > Mbps.
       - Pro Tip: It makes no sense to increase a video's data rate to a level that is higher than the data rate the video was originally recorded at. Why? It would simply increases the file size of the video and not increase its image quality.
       - Pro Tip: Mbps refers to *maximum* bits per second, not *mega* bits per second.
3. Deliver workspace > Custom Export > Advanced Settings > Data Levels:
   - Auto = sets data levels automatically based on the video codec used.
   - Video = shrinks the data levels to a safe level for broadcasting on television.
   - Full = sets the data levels to the absolute maximum. This setting uses all the image data available in the original video footage. (Please

Note: The internet and personal computers, as distinct from broadcast television, can play Full data rate levels in videos without any difficulty.)

4. Deliver workspace > Custom Export > Add to Render Queue
5. Deliver workspace > Render Queue (on right side) > Render All
   - A progress bar will appear to indicate how long the render (export) process will take.

Figure 121: Data Rate (Kb/s)

Figure 122: Chapter Markers

CHAPTER MARKERS

Chapter markers on a video can provide a convenient way for viewers to jump to a different chapter (or section) of a video, if they want. This can be useful for viewers to skip chapters or to replay other chapters. Chapter markers in DaVinci Resolve must be set up with a marker color placed on different sections of a video in a Timeline before export, and the markers used must all be of the same color. Quicktime (.mov) and .mp4 formats in DaVinci Resolve are the only formats that can export chapter markers. You can set up a video with chapter markers in DaVinci Resolve this way.

1. Position the playhead on a video clip in a Timeline where you want to add a chapter marker.
2. Press M
   - or Click the Marker icon at the top of the Timeline Toolbar.
3. Double click the marker to open it.
   A. Type in a marker (i.e., chapter) name.
   B. Give all the chapter markers the exact same color. This is required. Chapter markers only work when all of the chapter markers use the exact same color.
4. Repeat the above steps to add further chapter markers on different sections of the video.
5. Deliver workspace > Custom Export > Export Video > Format > Quicktime (.mov) or MP4 (.mp4).

6. Deliver workspace > Custom Export > Export Video > Click the Chapters from Markers checkbox on.
7. Deliver workspace > Custom Export > Export Video > Select the Color of the chapter markers used from the Color drop down menu (Figure 122).
8. Deliver workspace > Custom Export > Export Video > Add to Render Queue
9. Deliver workspace > Render Queue (on right side) > Render All
   - A progress bar will appear to indicate how long the render (export) process will take.

ALPHA CHANNEL

Exporting a video with an alpha channel (i.e., a transparent, see-through background) requires a fairly robust understanding of the different video export formats available for editors.

- ProRes 4444, DNxHD, and GoPro Cineform export formats all support alpha channels (i.e., transparent, see-through backgrounds) in DaVinci Resolve.
- H.264 and H.265 export formats do not support alpha channels.
- (For graphics files, .png graphics files support a transparent, see-through background whereas .jpg graphics files do not.)

You can find the alpha channel settings in DaVinci Resolve's Deliver workspace here.

1. Deliver workspace > Custom Export > Export Video > Format > Quicktime.
2. Deliver workspace > Custom Export > Export Video > Codec > Apple ProRes
3. Deliver workspace > Custom Export > Export Video > Type > Apple ProRes 4444
4. Deliver workspace > Custom Export > Export Video > Click the Export Alpha checkbox on.
5. Change the Alpha Channel Mode if needed.
   - Deliver workspace > Custom Export > Export Video > Alpha Mode > Premultiplied or Straight

CUSTOM EXPORT SETTINGS

You can customize and save your customized export settings for future reuse in DaVinci Resolve this way.

1. Deliver workspace > Custom Export > Set the export settings that you want on a video.
2. Deliver workspace > Custom Export > . . . (Options) drop down menu > Save as New Preset

RENDERING (CACHING)

———

Rendering and *caching* in DaVinci Resolve are the same thing, essentially. Video clips are *rendered* (or *cached*) in DaVinci Resolve so that they can be played back and edited more smoothly in a Timeline. Rendering eliminates the stuttering or choking effect that often accompanies compressed video clips or clips that have a lot of effects applied to them. DaVinci Resolve generates a completely new video copy (of the original video clip) during the rendering process and uses an optimized and uncompressed mezzanine format (typically a ProRes or DNxHD format) to render it with. Rendering format choices can be selected in DaVinci Resolve's render settings and the location of the folder containing the rendered video clip copies can be set in the Global (Preferences) and/or the Local (Settings) of DaVinci Resolve. (Please see the *Render Format* and *Render Files Folder Location* instructions provided below). The render folder should be placed on a fast external hard drive, if possible, and since the render files folder can become very large with multiple rendered video clip copies added to it, it should be deleted when a project is finally finished and exported in order to free up a computer's hard drive space. Deleting rendered video clip copies deletes the rendered video clip copies only in DaVinci Resolve; the original source video clips themselves remain; and the original source video clips can always be re-rendered, if needed, in the future.

RENDER FORMATS
You can choose the format used for rendering video clip copies in DaVinci Resolve (typically in an uncompressed mezzanine format) to ProRes on Apple computers, DNxHR on PC computers, or another format that you may choose. Both ProRes and DNxHR are very good and smooth render formats, but they can also create extremely large file sizes. They should be deleted from a computer's hard drive when a project is finally finished and exported, therefore. You can choose the format used for rendering video clip copies in DaVinci Resolve here.
- File > Project Settings > Master Settings > Optimized Media and Render Cache > Render Cache Format > Select either ProRes, DNxHR, or another

format for the rendered video clip copies that will be made. (ProRes and DNxHR are the preferred rendering formats.) (Figure 123)

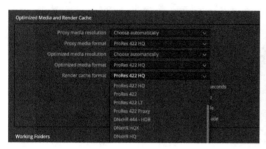

Figure 123: Render Format

Figure 124: Render Files Location

RENDER FILES FOLDER LOCATION

Render files (i.e., rendered video clip copies) should be placed in a folder on a fast external drive, if possible, in order to improve the playback performance of DaVinci Resolve. If the render files folder is placed on a computer's internal hard drive, it may fill up the hard drive quickly because rendered video clip copies are extremely large. They should be deleted, in turn, when a project is finally finished and exported in order to free up a computer's hard drive space. You can choose a render files folder location in DaVinci Resolve here.

1. File > Project Settings > Master Settings > Working Folders > Cache Files Location > CacheClip (default) or Browse and create a new folder location, if needed (Figure 124).
    - Pro Tip: You can also see DaVinci Resolve's render files folder locations here.
        - DaVinci Resolve Menu > Preferences > System > Media Storage

RENDERING MAY NOT BE NECESSARY

Some experienced video editors argue that rendering video clips in a DaVinci Resolve Timeline may not always be necessary. Rendering video clips can be a waste of a computer's processing power and a waste of an editor's valuable time while editing. It may be best, instead, to render only the final adjustments of an Effect on a video clip, as opposed to rendering each and every preliminary adjustment of an Effect, to limit the rendering process to only the essential rendering needed. In addition, rendering the entire video Timeline upon export may be a good option instead of rendering individual Effects or procedures in a Timeline beforehand. You can turn rendering on or off in DaVinci Resolve here.

- Playback Menu > Render Cache > None, Smart, User

AUTOMATIC BACKGROUND RENDERING

Automatic Background Rendering in DaVinci Resolve renders all video clips in a Timeline which DaVinci Resolve considers complicated and therefore in need of rendering. Simple video clips, by contrast, are not automatically rendered because simple video clips do not need to be rendered. Automatic Background Rendering starts, furthermore, when no activity in a Timeline happens (as when an editor pauses and thinks about how to edit, which is a very good way to approach editing). You can adjust the amount of time it takes for DaVinci Resolve to start Automatic Background Rendering from 5 seconds (the default) to any time here.

- File > Project Settings > Master Settings > Optimized Media and Render Cache > Click the Enable Background Caching After checkbox on and set the time to 1 Second or so.

RENDER PROGRESS BAR

DaVinci Resolve includes a render progress bar to show how long a rendering process will take and to show which video clips in a Timeline have already been rendered.

- A Red line appears above a rendered video clip in a Timeline in DaVinci Resolve to indicate *render is in progress.*
- A Blue line appears above a rendered video clip in a Timeline in DaVinci Resolve to indicate *render is complete.*

RENDER IN PLACE

Render in Place in DaVinci Resolve renders (or bakes in) a video clip's Effects, Titles, or Keyframes, etc., in a Timeline so that a video clip will playback smoothly without stuttering. An optimized and uncompressed copy of the video clip is generated in a ProRes or DNxHR mezzanine format, and this rendered video clip copy will play back smoothly and easily for editing. You can Render a video clip in Place in a Timeline in DaVinci Resolve this way.

- Right-click a video clip in a Timeline > Render in Place (Figure 125)
  - In the Render in Place dialog box that opens, select Format as Quicktime, Codec as Apple ProRes or DNxHR, and Type as Apple ProRes 422 or DNxHR HQ.

Figure 125: Render in Place | Figure 126: Use Rendered Clips on Export

MANUAL RENDERING

Manual Rendering – also known as User Rendering – renders a video clip in a Timeline in DaVinci Resolve that you select yourself and render individually.

1. First, set up the User Rendering options in DaVinci Resolve's settings here.
    - File > Project Settings > Master Settings > Optimized Media and Render Cache > Render Cache Format > Select either ProRes, DNxHR, or another format for the rendered video clip copies that will be made. (ProRes and DNxHR are the preferred rendering formats.)
        A. Click the Auto Cache Transitions in User Mode checkbox on.
        B. Click the Auto Cache Composites in User Mode checkbox on.
        C. Click the Auto Cache Fusion Effects in User Mode checkbox on.
2. Playback Menu > Render Cache > User
3. Right-click a video clip in a Timeline > Render Cache Fusion Output > Auto

EXPORT USING RENDER FILES

You can set up the Deliver workspace's render settings for export in DaVinci Resolve in 2 different ways.

1. With video clips that have already been rendered in a Timeline.
    - Deliver Page > Advanced Settings > Click the Use Render Cached Images checkbox on to export using the already rendered video clips in a Timeline (Figure 126).
2. With the original source video clips in DaVinci Resolve which have not been rendered.
    - Deliver Page > Advanced Settings > Leave the Use Render Cached Images checkbox unchecked to export using the original source video clips instead of the video clips that have already been rendered in a Timeline.

DELETE RENDER FILES

Rendered video clip copies in DaVinci Resolve can fill up a lot of hard drive space on a computer because rendered video clip copies generated in either ProRes or DNxHD mezzanine formats can be extremely large. When a project is finally finished and exported, therefore, all rendered video clip copies should be deleted from a computer's hard drive in order to free up disc space. Original source video clips will not be deleted in this process; only the rendered video clip copies will be deleted; and the original source video clips themselves can always be re-rendered again in the future in DaVinci Resolve, if needed. You can delete the rendered video clip copies generated in DaVinci Resolve this way.

- Playback Menu > Delete Render Cache > Choose either All, Unused, or Selected (Figure 127).
  - Pro Tip: You can also delete the rendered video clip copies generated in DaVinci Resolve manually by opening up the rendered video clip copies folder, selecting all the rendered video clip copies inside, and deleting them. You can find the rendered video clip copies folder in DaVinci Resolve here.
    - DaVinci Resolve Menu > Preferences > System > Media Storage (Figure 128)

Figure 127: Delete Render Files (when done)

Figure 128: Render Files Location

SETTINGS

—

2 KINDS OF SETTINGS IN DAVINCI RESOLVE

1. Global Settings. These are system-wide settings affecting all projects. You can find the Global Settings in DaVinci Resolve here.
   - DaVinci Resolve Menu > Preferences > System / User (Figure 129)
2. Local Settings. These are individual project settings affecting only one project at a time. New projects can have different project settings. You can find the Local Project Settings in DaVinci Resolve here.
   - File > Project Settings (Figure 130)
     - or Click the Settings (Gear) icon at the bottom right corner of the DaVinci Resolve user interface.
   - Pro Tip: Close and restart DaVinci Resolve in order to ensure that all new settings will go into effect.

Figure 129: Global Settings

Figure 130: Local (Project) Settings

LIVE SAVE (AUTO SAVE)

Live Save (a.k.a. Auto Save) automatically saves changes to projects every minute or so. Live Save safeguards against losing valuable work during a computer crash, for example. You do not have to keep selecting File > Save anymore, even though

File > Save is still available to use. You can set up Live Save (a.k.a. Auto Save) in DaVinci Resolve here.
- DaVinci Resolve Menu > Preferences > User > Project Save and Load > Click the Live Save checkbox on.

SPECIFIC SETTINGS
Please see the *Media Management, Rendering,* and *Improve Performance* chapters in *DaVinci Resolve Editing Step-By-Step Instructions* for explanations of how to adjust the settings found in each of these areas in DaVinci Resolve specifically.

CUSTOM SETTINGS
You can customize and save your own settings as user presets for later reuse in DaVinci Resolve this way.
1. File > Project Settings > Master Settings > Adjust any of the settings that you want.
2. Project Settings > . . . (Options) drop down menu > Save Current Settings as Preset
3. Name it.
4. Load a Custom Setting preset that you have saved in DaVinci Resolve this way.
   - File > Project Settings > Master Settings > . . . (Options) drop down menu > Select a Custom Setting that you have saved beforehand.

IMPROVE PERFORMANCE

DaVinci Resolve includes certain performance enhancing techniques that can allow it to operate more efficiently, if needed.

AUTO PERFORMANCE MODE
The Automatic Performance Mode in DaVinci Resolve automatically adjusts playback speed according to a computer's own CPU or GPU power, and it is ON by default. It will drop frames to keep playback running smoothly (eliminating video stuttering or choking) and the audio will remain smooth in the process. It also exports at the highest quality video settings set up in DaVinci Resolve's Project Settings. You can find the Automatic Performance Mode setting in DaVinci Resolve here.

- DaVinci Resolve Menu > Preferences > User > Playback Settings > Performance Mode > Automatic (ON by default)

STATUS DISPLAY
The Timeline Viewer's title bar contains a Status Display (i.e., a Frames Per Second counter) in its top left corner. This Status Display shows how many frames are being used when a video is playing, and it indicates if a computer is up to speed during playback or not. The Timeline Viewer's title also bar has a green and red LED indicator light that reveals satisfactory or unsatisfactory performance during playback. You can set up the Status Display controls in the Timeline Viewer in DaVinci Resolve here.

- Timeline Viewer > . . . (Options) drop down menu > Show All Video Frames = OFF (default).
  - This OFF setting (default) drops video frames whenever needed to maintain a steady playback in the Timeline Viewer.

- Timeline Viewer > . . . (Options) drop down menu > Show All Video Frames = ON.
  - This ON setting plays all video frames but may stutter or choke when a video is playing in the Timeline Viewer.
- 24 counter = no dropped frames in a video clip shot at 24 fps (17 = some dropped frames) (Figure 131).
  - Pro Tip: You can see a video clip's original frame rate when recorded in a camera, in order to compare it to the Timeline Viewer's playback of it, here.
    - A. Select a video clip in a Timeline.
    - B. Metadata (by Inspector) > Shot Frame Rate
- Green LED = a computer's GPU is sufficient.
- Red LED = a computer's GPU is insufficient.

Figure 131: Status Display (24 FPS Counter)

Figure 132: Timeline Resolution

TIMELINE PROXY RESOLUTION

The Timeline Proxy Resolution setting in DaVinci Resolve lowers a video's resolution on the fly in order to enhance real-time video playback and improve DaVinci Resolve's performance overall. It works independently from the *Proxy Media* feature (explained in the *Proxy Media* section of the *Media Management* chapter in *DaVinci Resolve Editing Step By Step Instructions*), even though the word *proxy* is included in this menu item. You do not have to create a proxy video clip copy in order to use this feature, that is. Timeline Proxy Resolution benefits from DaVinci Resolve's *resolution independent* operation, and while it may lower the sharpness of a video clip's playback in the Timeline Viewer a bit, the smoother playback will provide much better performance overall. You can find the Timeline Proxy Resolution control in DaVinci Resolve here.

- Playback Menu > Timeline Proxy Resolution > Full, Half, Quarter

TIMELINE RESOLUTION

The Timeline Resolution setting in DaVinci Resolve controls a Timeline's overall resolution. The two most common video resolution presets used today are UHD

(3840 x 2160) and HD (1920 x 1080). However, there are many other resolution presets available in DaVinci Resolve's Timeline Resolution setting, and you can even type in a custom resolution size if you want. DaVinci Resolve is a *resolution independent* editing platform, which means that a video's resolution can be changed at any time, differently sized videos can be imported into one Timeline, and multiple resolution versions of a video can be exported if needed. You can change the Timeline Resolution setting of a video in DaVinci Resolve here.

- File > Project Settings > Master Settings > Timeline Resolution (Figure 132)
  - Pro Tip: If your video clips were originally recorded in a camera at UHD (3840 x 2160), setting your Timeline Resolution in DaVinci Resolve to HD (1920 x 1080) can improve playback performance. (Powerful computers, of course, may not need to decrease the Timeline Resolution of a video from UHD [3840 x 2160] to HD [1920 x 1080], but slower computers may benefit from it.)
  - Pro Tip: All windows, tracks, sizing changes, and keyframe data are supposed to automatically recalculate when a video's Timeline Resolution is changed upon export. However, to be safe, you may want to first edit all video clips on an HD (1920 x 1080) Timeline and then change the Timeline to UHD (3840 x 2160) when you want to apply sizing changes or Keyframe data, etc., for a video's final export.
  - Pro Tip: In the Deliver workspace, when exporting a final video, you can have DaVinci Resolve use the already rendered video clips in an HD (1920 x1080) Timeline or use the original source UHD (3840 x 2160) video clips that have not been rendered. The original source UHD (3840 x 2160) video clips will be included in the final export instead of the video clips that have been rendered in the HD (1920 x 1080) Timeline.
  - Pro Tip: Ultimately, on slower computers, it may be helpful to shoot all video clips in a camera at HD (1920 x 1080), edit and render all Effects and procedures in an HD (1920 x 1080) Timeline, and then export the final video at HD (1920 x 1080) as well. Keeping everything at HD (1920 x 1080) from start to finish is a good workflow for professional filmmakers because an HD (1920 x 1080) resolution produces a high quality final video when exported and, of course, UHD (3840 x 2160) – though preferred – is not always necessary.
  - Pro Tip: Experimenting on test video clips on your own particular computer may be the best way to assess which performance enhancing techniques in DaVinci Resolve work best. Today's computers are mostly powerful enough to handle all of DaVinci Resolve's professional capabilities, but moderately powered computers, or older

computers, may benefit from some performance enhancing adjust-ments.

EXTERNAL VIDEO MONITOR

The External Video Monitor setting in DaVinci Resolve controls an external video monitor connected to a computer (like a large TV screen) in order to monitor a video on. It operates independently from DaVinci Resolve's Timeline and Source Viewer screens, and the settings it uses do not affect the video itself upon export. You can find the External Video Monitor settings in DaVinci Resolve here.

- File > Project Settings > Master Settings > Video Monitoring

DISABLE EXTRA TIMELINES

You can disable extra Timelines in the Media Pool, if any, to improve the perfor-mance of DaVinci Resolve this way.

- Media Pool > Right-click an extra Timeline > Disable Timeline

BYPASS COLOR / FUSION EFFECTS

You can bypass all Color and Fusion effects in a Timeline in DaVinci Resolve to improve performance this way.

- Click the Bypass icon at the top of the Timeline Viewer in DaVinci Resolve. It toggles "before" and "after" versions of all Color and Effect adjustments so that you can see how they look when applied. Leave this off while editing and turn it back on while exporting a video.
- You can also disable an Effect by clicking the red dot next to its title in the Inspector. Reenable an Effect (by clicking its red dot back on again) while exporting.

USE ADJUSTMENT CLIPS

You can apply Effects and Color grades to Adjustment Clips in DaVinci Resolve in order to improve performance as well.

1. Drag an Adjustment Clip to a Timeline in DaVinci Resolve.
   - Effects > Toolbox > Effects > Drag an Adjustment Clip to a layer above the other video clips a Timeline.
2. Effects > Open FX > Drag an Effect on top of the Adjustment Clip.
   - or Apply a color grade to the Adjustment Clip, if needed, in DaVinci Resolve's Color workspace.
3. Deactivate (and reactivate) the Adjustment Clip at any time.
   - Select the Adjustment Clip and press D to deactivate it.
   - Select the Adjustment Clip and press D again to reactivate it before export.

USE COMPOUND CLIPS

A Compound Clip flattens other video clips or layers of video clips into one video clip for easier maneuverability and processing. It can be reopened (i.e., decomposed) and re-edited at any time. You can create a compound clip on complicated video clips in a Timeline in DaVinci Resolve in order to improve performance this way.

1. Select a complicated video clip (or layers of complicated video clips) in a Timeline.
2. Right-click one of the video clips > New Compound Clip
3. Name it.
    - Pro Tip: You can render a Compound Clip to have it playback even more smoothly.
    - Right-click the compound video clip > Render in Place
4. You can reopen the compound video clip (i.e., decompose it) at any time in order to edit it further.
    - Right-click the compound video clip > Decompose in Place > Using Clips Only

MINIMIZE INTERFACE UPDATES

Minimizing the Interface Updates of DaVinci Resolve makes the On Screen Controls in the Timeline Viewer update only during pause and not during playback in order to help improve performance. You can minimize the Interface Update controls in DaVinci Resolve here.

- DaVinci Resolve Menu > Preferences > User > Playback Settings > Click the Minimize Interface Updates During Playback checkbox on.

HIDE INTERFACE OVERLAYS

Hiding the User Interface Overlays in DaVinci Resolve makes the On Screen Controls update only during pause and not during playback in order to help improve performance. You can find the Hide User Interface controls in DaVinci Resolve here.

- DaVinci Resolve Menu > Preferences > User > Playback Settings > Click the Hide UI Overlays checkbox on.

———

MEDIA MANAGEMENT

—

DATABASES

Databases in DaVinci Resolve are "folders" that contain everything a video needs to work with, except media assets and render files. Databases contain project files, timeline files, bins, metadata, and other information needed for a project. They are similar to the "libraries" used in Final Cut Pro editing software. Multiple projects and Timelines can also exist in one database. You should put a database on a computer's internal hard drive (since it is a relatively small text file containing just instructions), and put all media assets and render files used on a fast external drive (since media assets and render files can be extremely large).

- You can find a database in DaVinci Resolve here (Figure 132).
    - File > Project Manager > Click the database folder icon at the top left corner of the Project Page > Click the Information icon listed on it > Reveal in Finder.
- You can create a new database in DaVinci Resolve this way.
    - File > Project Manager > Click the Add Project Library button at the bottom left side of the Project Page.
- You can create a Back Up of a database in DaVinci Resolve this way.
    - File > Project Manager > Select a database > Click the Information icon listed on it > Back Up
- You can restore a database in DaVinci Resolve this way.
    - File > Project Manager > Select a database > Click the Restore icon above the database.

ENCODE

Encode refers to the process of compressing (i.e., "encoding") an uncompressed video clip (such as an uncompressed RAW video clip) to a compressed video for-

Figure 132: Databases

Figure 133: Plugin Management (p. 146)

mat. A video clip is "encoded" (i.e., compressed) to make it smaller and easier to share.

TRANSCODE

Transcode refers to the process of transferring an already compressed video clip into another compressed video clip format (such as "transcoding" a .mov video clip into an .mp4 video clip, or "transcoding" an H.265 video clip into an H.264 video clip). Both clips have been already compressed, but their formats are now changed for a different purpose.

OFFLINE EDITING

Offline Editing refers to the process of editing with generated proxy video clip "copies" in a Timeline instead of editing with the original, larger source video clips recorded in a camera. Offline Editing is usually used on low-powered computers to compensate for sluggish performance. However, RAW video workflows often generate smaller, proxy video clip copies to edit with as well because RAW video source clips are extremely large files and RAW video source clips themselves can be incompatible with some computers and NLEs today. Smaller proxy video clip copies are generated from the original high-resolution source video clips recoded in a camera, and they are generated in an uncompressed mezzanine format (typically a ProRes or DNxHD format) for smoother playback. When a video's editing is finally finished (using the proxy video clip "copies"), and when the video has been exported, the original high-resolution source video clips recorded in a camera should be used for export instead of the proxy video clip copies used during editing.

ONLINE EDITING

Online Editing refers to the process of editing a video with the original high-resolution source video clips recorded in a camera. It is usually used on high-powered computers because high-powered computers can edit large video files in an NLE's Timeline without much difficulty.

MISSING MEDIA

Missing Media is often referred to as *Offline Media* as well, but for a different reason. Missing Media (i.e., missing video clips or missing audio clips in a project) occurs when a folder containing a project's video clips or audio clips has been moved to a different location, or moved to a different external drive, or when the video clips or audio clips themselves have been renamed. DaVinci Resolve's link to them has been broken, and the video and audio clips, as a result, will need to be relinked. (Please see *Relink Media Files* explained below.)

RESOLUTION INDEPENDENCE

DaVinci Resolve is a *resolution independent* video editing program, meaning that its resolution settings can be flexible. For example, 4K and HD video clips can be imported into one Timeline together, the resolution of a Timeline can be changed at any time, and different resolutions of a video can be used for final export.

CODEC

A video *codec* makes a video small and manageable. Why? Videos are normally quite large and unmanageable. Video codecs compress videos in order to make them easier to export, stream, and/or share online. The word *codec* combines the words *compress* and *decompress* (exactly as the word *modem* combines the words *modulate* and *demodulate*). A video is first *compressed* in a codec to be shared online or elsewhere and then it is *decompressed* in a non-linear video editing (NLE) program on a computer in order to be edited. There are 2 basic kinds of video codecs available to filmmakers: *compressed* and *uncompressed*.

- *Compressed video codecs* compress videos for exporting and sharing. They make video clips small and easy to manage. However, compressed video clips can be difficult for some computers to decompress in a Timeline while editing and they can become sluggish, as a result. H.264 and the newer H.265 (High Efficiency Video Codec called HEVC) are widely used codecs today for exporting and sharing videos in, but some computers may not be able to decompress them very well during playback in a Timeline, and as a result, they can stutter or choke while editing. Compressed video codecs are designed for sharing as opposed to editing.
- *Uncompressed video codecs* (also known as *mezzanine* codecs) decompress videos in order to be edited smoothly in an NLE's Timeline. They are easy for computers to playback during editing because they do not have to be decompressed and played back at the same time. Nevertheless, uncompressed videos can have extremely large file sizes. A 1 GB H.264 video clip, for example, optimized to an uncompressed ProRes video file can be 4 times as large (at 4 GB). Apple's ProRes mezzanine video codec (typically used on

Macs) and Avid's DNxHD mezzanine video codec (typically used on PCs) operate very smoothly in a Timeline because they do not have to be decompressed while being played. Uncompressed video codecs are designed for editing as opposed to sharing.

- *H.264 video codec* is a codec that uses a predictive frame capturing process, meaning that it generates predicted copies of video frames in a video clip instead of recording each and every individual video frame specifically. It does this until a change in the video clip's movement or position occurs. The predictive frame capturing process, while creating a smaller-sized video in the end, may be difficult for some computers to play back because it requires a computer to generate the predicted frames while playing the video at the same time.
- *ALL-I (ALL-Intraframe) video codec* is a codec that captures each and every video frame of a video clip as separate and individual video frames – it records *all* of the individual video frames of a video clip – and it is a preferred video codec for professional video editors. ProRes and DNxHD codecs use the ALL-I frame capturing process, and the H.264 video codec can actually use the ALL-I frame capturing process if it is available in a camera's settings. The ALL-I frame capturing process produces a larger file size than the predictive frame capturing process, but it produces a smoother workflow for video editors.

FORMAT

A video *format* is also known as a "container format." It contains the video codec, the audio codec, the metadata, the subtitles, and all of the other items that are needed for a video to operate. It contains everything needed in a video, whereas a video *codec* contains just the video's compressing and decompressing information.

- .mov (Apple's Quicktime movie format) and .mp4 are some of the most popular and reliable video "container formats" available for filmmakers today.
- Both the .mov and .mp4 container formats can include the H.264, H.265, ProRes, and DNxHD video codecs used today.
- .mp4 (MPEG-4) is an International container format that does not contain DRM (Digital Rights Management) protections, which prevent unlawful copying and piracy. Nevertheless, .mp4 is a widely used container format for Macs, PCs, and mobile devices, as well as commonly streamed on the internet. It works reliably on both Macs and PCs.
- .m4v (which is not the same thing as .mp4) is another Apple container format and it includes DRM (Digital Rights Management) protocols to prevent

unlawful copying and piracy; however, .m4v is not as widely used as the .mov and .mp4 container formats.

- Pro Tip: VLC, Handbrake, and Quicktime video player software programs can convert H.265 (HEVC) video clips into traditional H.264 video clips for smoother playback in NLEs used today. You can open up an H.265 (HEVC) video in one of the above mentioned player software programs and export it as an H.264 video instead. Other video converter programs can be searched for on the internet and used for converting videos as well.
- Pro Tip: DaVinci Resolve supports the following video and graphics file formats, among many others: AVI, Cineon, DCP, DPX, IMF, EXR, JPEG2000, MJ2, MP4 (.mp4), QUICKTIME (.mov), and TIFF. DaVinci Resolve, as a professional non-linear video editing software program, can also export 3-D movie formats, Digital Cinema Project (DCP) files for distribution to digital cinemas, and several of today's professional streaming service requirements such as Netflix, using Netflix's own presets and protocols, among other formats.

ALPHA CHANNEL

An *Alpha Channel* is the part of a video clip that contains a transparent (i.e., a see-through) background. However, if a video clip with an Alpha Channel does not display its transparent background properly, you can always change the video clip's Alpha Channel settings in DaVinci Resolve to correct it here.

- Media Pool > Right-click a video clip with an Alpha Channel > Clip Attributes > Video > Alpha Mode > None, Premultiply, Invert, Straight.

MEDIA PREPARATION

Media Management *per se* involves the management of media assets (i.e., video clips, audio clips, and graphics files) before they get imported into DaVinci Resolve for editing. Good media management can save a video editor a lot of trouble in working with media files in the editing or exporting processes of filmmaking later on. Media Management specifically involves naming media with descriptive names, giving the folders they are in descriptive names as well, and placing the folders of the media in a location on a computer that is easy to find. There is a popular expression heard in film school: "A good filmmaker is a well-prepared filmmaker." In the same way, good media management (i.e., "preparing" media assets before import) can save a video editor a lot of trouble in filmmaking later on.

- Pro Tip: In order to prepare well before editing a video in DaVinci Resolve, a video editor would do well to place all video clips in a folder on a computer and then rename the video clips inside the folder specific names (such as beach1, people2, train3, etc). Give the folder that the video clips are in a descriptive name as well (such as *GH4 beach 02 14 23*). Place the folder on a fast external drive, if possible, and copy the folder onto a second external drive as a back up. You can delete these folders in the future when they are no longer needed or move them to a bulk external drive for long-term storage.

- Pro Tip: The Finder window on a Mac has a Batch Rename feature that can rename multiple video clips and other media files all at once. You can select similar video clips inside a folder (such as beach video clips) by command clicking non-contiguous video clips, and then rename all of them *Beach*, for example. The name *Beach* will precede each video clip's name with the original file name retained after it. In addition, you can add a letter "a" in front of the names of your best video clips so that they will be repositioned at the top of a folder as a high priority. When you import these video clips into DaVinci Resolve, they will appear in alphabetical order in the Media Pool and they will be easy to find and recognized. (Video clips with the color labels from the Finder's color tag feature on a Mac do not show up as color-labeled video clips in the Media Pool in DaVinci Resolve. However, you can always color-code a video clip in the Media Pool or in a Timeline in DaVinci Resolve this way.)
    - Right-click a video clip in the Media Pool or a Timeline > Clip Color

PLUGIN MANAGEMENT

DaVinci Resolve allows a video editor to access and control video and audio plugins that may have been purchased online and installed on a computer to increase the functionality of DaVinci Resolve. You can manage and see different video and audio plugins in DaVinci Resolve here (Figure 133).

- DaVinci Resolve Menu > Preferences > System > Video Plugins / Audio Plugins > Enable All / Disable All, Add / Remove / Save

MEDIA MANAGEMENT COMMAND

DaVinci Resolve allows a video editor to move, copy, transcode, and/or remove media in a project through the Media Management Command. The Media Management Command can even transcode video files in more formats than those listed in DaVinci Resolve's Deliver workspace. You can use the Media Management Command in DaVinci Resolve this way.

1. Media Pool > Select a Timeline
2. File > Media Management Command > Select Copy or Transcode > Destination (Figure 134)

CLIP ATTRIBUTES

Clip Attributes is a panel in DaVinci Resolve's Media Pool that provides information on video and audio clips used in a project. It also allows a video editor to adjust some of a video or audio clip's internal settings if a change is needed to get a video or audio clip to operate more effectively in a Timeline. You can find the Clip Attributes panel in DaVinci Resolve here.

- Media Pool > Right-click a video or audio clip > Clip Attributes > Video, Audio, Timecode, Name (Figure 135)

Figure 134: Media Management Command   Figure 135: Clip Attributes

INSPECTOR > FILE

The File tab in the Inspector in DaVinci Resolve contains important metadata information about a selected video or audio clip, or a graphics file, in the Media Pool or a Timeline. You can find the Inspector > File feature here.

1. Select a video, audio, or a graphics file in the Media Pool or a Timeline.
2. Inspector > File tab
   - or Metadata (near Inspector)

INSPECTOR > IMAGE

The Image tab in the Inspector in DaVinci Resolve allows a video editor to change a RAW photo's overall features and settings. You can find the Inspector > Image feature in DaVinci Resolve here.

1. Select a RAW file in the Media Pool or a Timeline.
2. Inspector > Image tab

RELINK MISSING MEDIA FILES

Missing Media (i.e., missing video clips or audio clips in a project) may occur when a folder that contains video clips or audio clips has been moved to a different location, or moved to a different external drive, or when the video clips or audio clips themselves have been renamed. DaVinci Resolve's link to them has been broken, and as a result, the media files will need to be relinked. You can Relink Missing Media Files in DaVinci Resolve this way.

1. Edit workspace > Media Pool > Click the Relink Media icon at the top of the Media Pool (Figure 136).
2. Click the Locate button in the dialog box that appears and browse for the approximate folder that the video clips were originally placed in.
3. Select the folder on the hard drive where the video clips were originally placed.
4. DaVinci Resolve will scan all of the video or audio clips inside the folder and automatically relink the missing video or audio clips in the Media Pool.
    - Please Note: You can select the Disk Search button in the Relink Media dialog box as well to have DaVinci Resolve search an entire hard drive on a computer, but this will take a long time to work and it is not advised.
        - Pro Tip: If the steps above don't work, you can manually search for the original video or audio clips on a computer and re-import them into the Media Pool a second time.

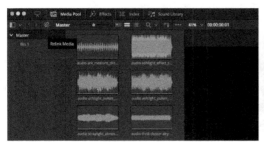 

Figure 136: Relink Missing Media   Figure 137: Copy a Timeline to a 2nd Computer

COPY TIMELINE TO A SECOND COMPUTER

DaVinci Resolve allows a video editor to copy a Timeline from one computer (at home, for example) to another computer (at an office or school) if so desired. The same media assets (video clips, audio clips, and/or graphics files) used in the project on the first computer must also be copied onto the second computer for this to work, and they must also be imported into the second computer's Media Pool. You can copy a Timeline to a second computer in DaVinci Resolve this way.

1. Media Pool > Select the Timeline of the project you are working on.
2. File > Export > Timeline (a DaVinci Resolve Timeline has a .drt file extension.) (Figure 137)
3. Where > Desktop (or a preferred location)
4. Copy the .drt Timeline file (and its media assets) onto a second computer.
5. Import the Timeline into the second computer.
    A. Select the Media Pool in DaVinci Resolve on the second computer.

B. File > Import Timeline
C. Select the .drt file added from the first computer and import it. It should link up well with the same media assets (video clips, audio clips, and/or graphics files) that have been copied over from the first computer as well and imported into the Media Pool on the second computer.
- Pro Tip: Copying a Project to a second computer works similarly well.
- File > Export Project

OPTIMIZED MEDIA

Optimized Media in DaVinci Resolve refers to copies of original source video clips *optimized* (or "transcoded") into an easily editable uncompressed mezzanine codec (such as ProRes or DNxHR). These optimized video clip copies provide easier playback during editing. They remove the stuttering or choking effect that normally accompanies compressed video clips (such as H.265 or H.264 video clips) or video clips that have become challenged for other reasons. (Please Note: Some video editors find that H.264 or H.265 video clips work very well on their own in a Timeline and do not need to be optimized.) Nevertheless, optimized media files of uncompressed video clip copies can be very large, and they can take up a lot of space on a computer's hard drive, especially if a lot of them are generated. Therefore, deleting the optimized media files when a project is finally finished and exported is important in order to free up a computer's disc space. You can generate optimized video clip copies of your original source video clips for smoother playback in DaVinci Resolve this way.

1. File > Project Settings > Master Settings > Optimized Media and Render Cache > Optimized Media Resolution > Choose Automatically, Half, Quarter, One-Eighth size, etc (Figure 138).
   A. File > Project Settings > Master Settings > Optimized Media and Render Cache > Optimized Media Format > Select ProRes, DNxHR, or another file format for the optimized video clip copies that will be made.
   B. File > Project Settings > Master Settings > Working Folder > Cache Files Location > CacheClip or Browse.
2. Media Pool > Right-click a video clip > Generate Optimized Media
3. Playback Menu > Use Optimized Media if Available (Figure 139)
4. Set export settings upon the final export of a video.
   - Deliver Page > Advanced Settings > Select Use Optimized Media for export.
5. Delete the optimized media files when a project is finally finished and exported.

- Playback Menu > Delete Render Cache > All, Unused, Selected Clips

Figure 138: Create Optimized Media

Figure 139: Use Optimized Media

PROXY MEDIA

Proxy Media in DaVinci Resolve refers to the generation of smaller video clip copies of a camera's original source video clips in order to make editing easier and smoother in a Timeline. They are copies made with uncompressed mezzanine codecs (such as ProRes or DNxHD) in smaller resolution sizes for effortless editing and trouble-free operation. The editing process using proxy media file copies of original source video clips is called *offline editing*. When a project is finally finished, the project can be exported using the original source video clips recorded in a camera instead of the proxy media file copies edited in the Timeline. This will ensure that a full-sized and high-quality video will be exported. RAW video workflows typically create and edit proxy media (video clip copies) for editing because RAW video clips are extremely large to work with and RAW video clips may also be incompatible with some computers and NLEs today. The proxy media file copies should be deleted when a project is finally finished and exported to free up a computer's hard drive space. You can generate proxy media file copies of a camera's original source video clips in DaVinci Resolve this way.

1. File > Project Settings > Master Settings > Optimized Media and Render Cache > Proxy Media Resolution > Choose Automatically, Half, Quarter, or One-Eight size, etc.
    A. File > Project Settings > Master Settings > Optimized Media and Render Cache > Proxy Media Format > Select ProRes, DNxHR, or another file format for the proxy video clip copies that will be made.
    B. File > Project Settings > Master Settings > Working Folders > Proxy Generation Location > default location or Browse.
2. Media Pool > Right-click a video clip > Generate Proxy Media
3. Playback Menu > Proxy Handling > Prefer Proxies
4. Set export settings upon the final export of a video.

- Deliver Page > Advanced Settings > Leave the Use Proxy Media checkbox unchecked so the original (large) video files will be exported.

5. Delete the proxy video clip copies when a project is finally finished and exported.
    - Playback Menu > Delete Render Cache > All, Unused, Selected Clips

VFX CONNECT

DaVinci Resolve allows a video editor to "roundtrip" a video clip in a Timeline to the stand-alone Fusion Studio application to have professional special effects work or motion graphics work applied to it. A video editor can then re-import the video clip back from the stand-alone Fusion Studio application into DaVinci Resolve when the work is done. You can find the VFX Connect feature in DaVinci Resolve here.

1. Right-click a video clip in DaVinci Resolve > New VFX Connect Clip
2. Select the Format and Codec to use, etc., in the VFX Connect dialog box that appears.

ARCHIVE A PROJECT

DaVinci Resolve allows a video editor to archive a project when a project is finally finished and exported in order to store it away for safe keeping. The project file and the media files are included in the archived project, so the archived project can be quite large. However, you can always delete a project's render files first in order to make the archived project smaller and free up space on a computer's hard drive. (Render files can always be re-generated later in DaVinci Resolve, if needed.) You can archive a project in DaVinci Resolve this way.

- File > Project Manager > Right-click a Project > Export Project Archive

———

www.ingramcontent.com/pod-product-compliance
Lightning Source LLC
LaVergne TN
LVHW081529050326
832903LV00025B/1695